Face to Face

**CORWIN
PRESS**

The Corwin Press logo—a raven striding across an open book—
represents the happy union of courage and learning. We are a
professional-level publisher of books and journals for K–12 educators, and we are committed to creating and providing resources
that embody these qualities. Corwin's motto is "Success for All
Learners."

Face to Face

Communication and Conflict Resolution in the Schools

Philip S. Morse
Allen E. Ivey

CORWIN PRESS, INC.
A Sage Publications Company
Thousand Oaks, California

For information address:

Corwin Press, Inc.
A Sage Publications Company
2455 Teller Road
Thousand Oaks, California 91320
e-mail: order@corwin.sagepub.com

SAGE Publications Ltd.
6 Bonhill Street
London EC2A 4PU
United Kingdom

SAGE Publications India Pvt. Ltd.
M-32 Market
Greater Kailash I
New Delhi 110 048 India

Printed in the United States of America

Library of Congress Cataloging-in-Publication Data

Morse, Philip S.
    Face to face : communication and conflict resolution in the schools / Philip S. Morse, Allen E. Ivey.
       p.   cm.
    Includes bibliographical references
    ISBN 0-8039-6307-6 (alk. paper). — ISBN 0-8039-6308-4 (pbk. : alk. paper)
    1. Communication in education. 2. Teacher-student relationships. 3. Conflict management. I. Ivey, Allen E. II. Title.
LB1033.5.M67   1996
371.1'022—dc20   96-5103

This book is printed on acid-free paper.

96   97   98   99   00   10   9   8   7   6   5   4   3   2   1

Corwin Press Production Editor: S. Marlene Head

Contents

Foreword

Face to Face: Communication and Conflict Resolution in the Schools goes directly to the heart of conflict in human relationships. Understanding why conflicts arise and how they can be peacefully resolved among people are global issues for the 1990s and beyond. Conflicts between people have been an ongoing part of the evolutionary process of human beings for tens of thousands of years. Conflicts arise from the most basic human needs, which have been described by Abraham Maslow as physiological, safety, belongingness, esteem, self-actualization, desire to know, and aesthetic needs (Maslow, 1943). As authors Philip Morse and Allen Ivey state in the first chapter of *Face to Face*,

> Few reformers would suggest that schools should spend all their time and energies dealing with the emotional needs and concerns of students. However, most reformers would agree that we should first attend to some basic needs before we can seriously address the more complex sophisticated learning tasks that face students. (p. 1)

Research in inner-city schools demonstrates that safe, productive, and caring learning environments begin with positive and effective communication (Rogers & Freiberg, 1994). Students seem to bring fewer of these positive communication skills to classrooms each year. Put-downs, killer statements, and the latest word, "diss"-ing (indicating disrespect for another), are becoming the norm rather than the exception. In one urban middle school with nearly 1,300 students, 388 students were sent to the office to be disciplined during the month of October. However, when repeat referrals were added, the number of instances equaled 894 referrals to the office for one month (Freiberg, Stein, & Parker, 1995). If we agree that these are unacceptable conditions for learning, then we must ask ourselves, What are workable alternatives?

Face to Face: Communication and Conflict Resolution in the Schools provides both processes and approaches to the overall improvement of the climate and learning environments of schools. Much of what we see as discipline problems in classrooms and schools relate to breakdowns in communication. Improving communication is the focus of *Face to Face*. Morse and Ivey bring to the reader more than 50 years of their collective experience in counseling and teaching. They provide a framework of principles and strategies to guide teachers, students, parents, and administrators in more effective face-to-face communication while using the same principles to teach conflict resolution.

The authors incorporate a "microskills" model that builds from both microteaching and microcounseling. This model emphasizes communication and listening skills, primary prerequisites to effective communication. Microteaching initially was developed for teacher educators to assist new teachers in the acquisition of specific teaching actions to improve instruction. It worked for veteran teachers by refining and expanding teaching repertoires. By focusing on unique and alterable teaching skills, it makes transfer to the classroom more likely to occur. Microcounseling techniques were developed by Allen Ivey to enable counselors and other educators to construct meaningful strategies for carrying out their approaches to resolving conflicts. The microskills model is the thread that Morse and Ivey have used very effectively to weave the understanding of thoughts and feelings of others into your communication framework. Communication begins with listening to and understanding other people's ideas. According to Morse and Ivey, "It is the interchange between listening and influencing, pacing and leading, that is essential to conflict negotiation and mediation" (p. 6).

The chapters clearly describe specific interpersonal skills that are important to creating safe and caring learning environments and resolving conflicts once they occur. These skills, ranging from attending through confronting, provide the reader with ideas and strategies that are easily translatable to actions. "Win-win" solutions are encouraged through problem solving on both an individual and schoolwide basis. Teachers and administrators will find this book to be an important tool for responding to the breakdown of relationships in the classroom and preventing and resolving conflicts that arise in schools.

The resolution of conflicts can be a measure of either the advancement and development of a society, civilization, or species, or its limitations. Violence on an individual scale and war on a group, national, or global scale are perhaps the most recognizable responses to conflict. Peaceful resolutions to conflict have been rarely chronicled unless as a conclusion to war. In the 20th century, peace has been known almost solely as the interval between wars.

Although there is some research to indicate that a few people may be predisposed toward violence, most of the ways we respond to conflict are learned from our environment. In modern times, these responses are learned in the home, school, community, and religious organizations, and from peers and the media. If these sources all gave the same message of peaceful responses to conflicts, this and other books about conflict resolution would not be needed. Unfortunately, the message primary children receive today about how to resolve conflicts—mostly from the media but also from the home—is one based on violence.

Juvenile arrests are up 30-fold since 1950, and projections show a doubling of crimes committed by youth over the next 20 years. Given the current instability of families, reduced religious attendance, highly mobile communities, and violence as the norm for resolving conflicts, schools may provide the only opportunity students have to receive a positive message about resolving conflicts (Freiberg, Stein, & Huang, 1995).

Face to Face: Communication and Conflict Resolution in the Schools is a timely response to the urgent need for resolving escalating violence among American youth. Parents, teachers, students, administrators, teacher educators, and business and community leaders will find this book to be a valuable source for violence prevention and intervention. Many people who play dual roles as educator and parent will find this book very helpful in understanding and communicating with their own children. It takes an entire community to create safe, caring, and productive learning environments.

Knowing how to prevent and resolve conflicts should be the highest priority of all near and far members of a community.

Schools are the testing ground for children and youth who are trying to find their way in the world. Conflict among children is natural and begins at an early age. Conflicts will always arise, but the key to social harmony is how we resolve those conflicts. Parents, teachers, and community members can all be positive role models in both preventing conflicts through face-to-face communication and providing alternatives to violence. This book provides important prevention and mediation alternatives for those in the helping professions.

Morse and Ivey state that "Excellence in education requires masterful communication: the ability to listen and learn, to focus and confront, and to lead and influence others" (p. 8). The ultimate significance of *Face to Face: Communication and Conflict Resolution in the Schools* is its ability to raise our personal level of awareness of the importance of finding specific ways to create positive communication in schools and classrooms and in our own lives.

H. JEROME FREIBERG
University of Houston, Texas

References

Freiberg, H. J., Stein, T. A., & Huang, S. (1995). The effects of a classroom management intervention on student achievement in inner-city elementary schools. *Education Research and Evaluation, 1*(1), 36-66.

Freiberg, H. J., Stein, T. A., & Parker, G. (1995). An examination of discipline referrals in an urban middle school. *Education & Urban Society, 27*(4), 421-440.

Maslow, A. (1943). A theory of human motivation. *Psychological Review, 50*, 370-396.

Rogers, C. R., & Freiberg, H. J. (1994). *Freedom to learn* (3rd ed.). Columbus, OH: Merrill.

Acknowledgments

We would like to thank Mary Finn, who helped make chapter 9 a reality with her encyclopedic knowledge of the leading conflict resolution curricula programs, and Ron Andrea, whose prior collaborative efforts on peer mediation helped in the writing of chapter 8.

Our thanks also to Mary Bradford Ivey, the Amherst Regional Schools, Professor Ernest Washington, the University of Massachusetts, and Bertit Bratt, Bratt Institute, Sweden.

We gratefully acknowledge the assistance of Charlotte R. Morse and Margaret B. Morse, who helped in scrutinizing the syntax and overall clarity of the text. Our gratitude also to the teacher coordinators, Robert Grant and Stephen Monks, of the Greece Athena peer mediation program in Greece, New York for making their materials available to us.

We also are indebted to some of the teachers in the San Francisco Bay area, particularly Cindi Calimpong and Paddy Gutierrez, for letting us videotape and transcribe a few of their teaching moments.

And finally, we would like to acknowledge the contribution of the students we interviewed at School #43 of the Buffalo City Schools, who helped us fully grasp what kinds of violence children face in their lives. In addition, we can only express how moved we were to see just how good some of the School #43 peer mediators became in resolving conflicts, demonstrating all the communication and conflict-resolution skills that anyone could expect of them, and then some.

PHILIP S. MORSE
ALLEN E. IVEY

About the Authors

Philip S. Morse is a Professor in the Education Department at the State University of New York College of Fredonia. He is the coauthor of two books, *Young Children at Home and in School: 212 Educational Activities for Their Parents, Teachers, and Caregivers*, and *Home-Style Learning: Activities for Young Children and Their Parents*. He has published extensively on the subjects of communication and conflict-resolution skills, early childhood education, and the teaching of writing.

Morse has conducted more than 100 consultations and presentations to international groups, national and state conferences, and local organizations and schools. He has held appointments as a visiting scholar at the Graduate School of Education at the University of California at Berkeley and Harvard University and is presently a trainer for the Alternatives to Violence Program (AVP). He is also affiliated with Alternatives to Violence in Schools (AViS) and the Western New York Peace Center and is presently a consultant to schools that desire to set up peer mediation programs. A trainer for the Alternatives to Violence Program (AVP), he is also a volunteer mediator/arbitrator for the Better Business Bureau.

Allen E. Ivey is Distinguished University Professor in the School and Counseling Psychology Program at the University of Massachusetts, Amherst. He also is president of Microtraining Associates, Inc.

Ivey earned his A.B. from Stanford University in 1955. After a year as a Fulbright Scholar at the University of Copenhagen, Denmark, he completed his Ed.D. at Harvard University in 1959. Ivey, a Diplomate of the American Board of Professional Psychology in counseling psychology, is past president of the Division of

Counseling Psychology of the American Psychological Association. He has lectured widely in North America and internationally.

In addition, Ivey is the author or coauthor of 21 books and nearly 200 articles and chapters in books, and his works have been translated into 13 languages. His most recent book, *Counseling and Psychotherapy: Multicultural Perspectives*, illustrates how to integrate multicultural theory with traditional psychodynamic, cognitive-behavioral, and humanistic thought.

Epigraph

—All of us who are working in the field of human relationships and trying to understand the basic orderliness of that field are engaged in the most crucial enterprise in today's world. If we are thoughtfully trying to understand our tasks as administrators, teachers, educational counselors, vocational counselors, therapists, then we are working on the problem which will determine the future of this planet. For it is not upon the physical sciences that the future will depend. It is upon us who are trying to understand and deal with the interaction between human beings—who are trying to create helping relationships. (p. 57)

Rogers, C. R. (1961). *On becoming a person*. Boston: Houghton Mifflin.

1

The Listening Teacher
and Administrator

Education is a profoundly human enterprise. Reaching students both as learners and as maturing individuals with all their fears, joys, and occasional difficulties is a daunting task. Two of the biggest challenges both teachers and administrators face in schools today are how to communicate effectively with their students and how to resolve conflicts among them. This book addresses the communication skills and conflict resolution principles one needs for the smooth functioning of schools and effective teaching of students.

Suggestions for change in our schools inevitably focus on addressing basic needs of children—the need for children to feel safe and secure in school, not to come to school hungry, to feel cared about, and to feel at ease with themselves and others. For several years parents have identified violence in the schools and the safety of their children in schools as a top concern and priority (Elam, Rose, & Gallup, 1994; Johnson & Immerwahr, 1994-1995). Few reformers would suggest that schools should spend all their time and energies dealing with the emotional needs and concerns of students. However, most reformers agree that we should first attend to some basic needs before we can seriously address the more complex and sophisticated learning tasks that face students.

The idea of teaching children to care has had increasing support from a number of sources (Himmelfarb, 1994-1995; Kohn, 1991; Noddings, 1995; Rogers & Freiberg, 1994). Caring in the curriculum deals not only with the need for basic respect for others but with responding to the "growing emotional 'neediness' of many students—the result of a diminished adult presence and increased stress and violence in many students' lives" (Wagner, 1995, p. 395).

If one embraces the need for a school environment that is more secure, less violent, and more caring, then one must talk about the tools for dealing with such issues—how human beings can communicate effectively with one another and also learn the problem-solving skills of conflict resolution and strategies leading to alternatives to violence. If teachers and administrators are often in an adversarial relationship with students, then we must ask what processes and approaches are available for improving the overall atmosphere and environment of the school.

The helping professions have extensively documented the techniques used by counselors, social workers, clergy, substance abuse workers, attorneys, physicians, nurses, and others to communicate successfully with their clients. More and more, educators and other professionals are finding that the communication skills of the helping professions are ones that are universally applicable in any interactive relationship where one person seeks the help of another. Counselors and other professional helpers have spoken of the desirability of using counseling skills in contexts other than their own profession (Ivey, 1974; Kahn & Kahn, 1990; Kottler & Kottler, 1993; Pelsma, 1987; Rogers & Freiberg, 1994; Rosen, 1982; Rothwell, 1984).

Spear (1978) states,

> By emphasizing the purely personal dimension of technique, training in counseling skills would help teachers identify the strengths of their own personal styles and modify or develop classroom methods most complementary to them. Finally, training of this sort pulls into the teaching situation the most fundamental goal of counseling and psychotherapy—an increase in students' ability to discover, verbalize, and communicate ideas of great concern to them. (p. 374)

The helping professions have long known that the way one communicates is closely related to what is communicated. The best-intentioned therapist or social worker will be discounted or even dismissed as a helping agent if he or she threatens or otherwise does not help the client. Consequently, anyone whose professional responsibility is to help another person inevitably learns that certain communication patterns are more effective than others.

In spite of the need to master these techniques, one of the least discussed areas in preservice programs and inservice workshops is the impact of both verbal and nonverbal communication skills on students and staff alike. In this book we would like to describe not only those communication skills and techniques that make for a safe, secure, productive, and joyful classroom environment but also how they can be applied. We realize that those skills can be put to good use, not only in the environment of the classroom and school but in helping foster an atmosphere where less strife, aggressiveness, and tension exist.

It is difficult to teach in a classroom where students are bored, challenging the teacher's authority, or continually in conflict with one another. One of the most prevalent fears of beginning teachers is whether or not they will be able to control their new classes— whether or not students who disrupt the classroom can be controlled. What we shall attempt to do is to provide a framework of some principles and techniques to guide students, parents, teachers, and administrators so that they can communicate effectively with one another and at the same time use these principles in teaching conflict resolution effectively. In addition, we shall try to show how the basic elements of good communication skills can enhance concepts like teaching for thinking and understanding.

Principles of Quality Learning

A brief review of some basic ideas for what many consider to be fundamental principles behind quality learning will reveal that good communication skills and a conflict-free environment are inherent in many of them (Morse & Brand, 1995).

1. Students do better as active, engaged learners rather than playing the role of passive vessels waiting to be filled. From the time of John Dewey, and as far back as Pestalozzi

and Froebel, educators have talked about the desirability of the student's being an active, crucial agent in the learning process. And there are people in the student's environment who can help make sense out of what the student is investigating and learning. For example, cooperative learning involves peers and teachers communicating effectively with the student in the absence of conflict.

2. Learning is a natural, lifelong process that involves an integrated, holistic approach. Although some learning can be a solo activity, such as a child lost in wonder at a colony of beetles she sees on the ground before her, much reinforcement and eventual understanding come from the sensitive reinforcement by adults around her. For instance, a teacher who can skillfully ask the right questions and provide the proper focus can do much to aid the natural progress a child achieves in making sense out of the world's often-bewildering buzz of confusion. Again, nonverbal and verbal communication skills can do much in a teacher's total effectiveness with his or her students.

3. Adults are strong role models for children of all ages. Much has been written about the most effective role of the teacher in the classroom. Although disseminator of information has been the historically defined role for the teacher, more and more authorities are now suggesting that the teacher as facilitator can better support and nurture the student as an effective learner (Rogers & Freiberg, 1994). Implicit in the definition of teacher as facilitator are individuals who possess a complete repertoire of the communication skills presented in this book.

4. Research has shown that effective principals often have good interpersonal skills and can communicate effectively with school personnel, parents, and students. In addition, the concept of the principal as a head teacher offers much as a model for effective school management and curriculum reform.

One of the most important traits of an effective teacher and role model is that the individual know how to create a positive learning environment and help the student feel accepted, included, and successful. Aspy and Roebuck (1977), in a large study of teachers and students, identified a positive correlation between the utilization of effective communication strategies and student achievement, improved attendance, fewer disciplinary problems, gains on creativity scores, increased scores on self-concept measures, greater spontaneity, and higher levels of thinking.

When college students were asked in a survey what they valued in their K-12 teachers and for suggestions on how to become first-rate teachers, almost two thirds replied that good teachers respect children and relate to them on a personal level. Many also mentioned the ability to listen as a positive and desirable trait in excellent teachers. In essence, the survey showed that schools work best for students when students feel a human connection with a caring, genuine, interested, supportive, empathetic, and respectful teacher (Morse, 1994, p. 136).

Pacing and Leading:
Two Important Communication Strategies

We shall divide communication skills into two categories: "pacing" and "leading." In pacing your communication, you learn to listen to and walk with the person with whom you are interacting. As a teacher, your first task is to understand "where your students are." You need to learn how they think and what they need. In short, teaching needs to be based on listening to the student and pacing where they start.

An administrator also needs to pace. Before taking administrative action with a parent, student, or staff member, it is vital to enter the world of the other person. Pacing skills taught in this book (attending behavior, questioning, reflecting, and focusing skills) all relate to "walking with" and understanding the other person.

Leading is an equally important skill and one we tend to focus on most often in teaching and administration. Leading, as a skill, is a natural offshoot of skilled listening and pacing. Once you have moved in step with the other person, child or adult, you can then move with them and skillfully lead them in new directions. The influencing skills of communication that come into play here include interpretation or reframing, self-disclosure, advice, and

direction. Also, that central skill of teaching—providing information clearly so that it is heard—is an important influencing skill.

The caring attitude is central to this book. Unless you care and
are committed to students and the educational profession, the
highly specific ideas and skills of this book will be only partially
effective. *Face to Face: Communication and Conflict Resolution in the
Schools* presents the "how to" of successful communication. However, to this "how to" we must add the personal dimension—you
and your interest in students and education.

Microskills: The Backbone of Pacing and Leading

Just what is effective communication? What does it look like?
Can it be broken down into manageable units? Can it be taught? The
answer to these and other questions has been examined for the past
30 years within the counseling framework of "microcounseling"
and "microskills." More than 300 data-based studies attest to the
usefulness of the microskills model (Baker & Daniels, 1989; Daniels
& Ivey, in press).

The microskills model is adapted from "microteaching" and focuses on specific teachable units. Where the microteaching model
focuses on information giving, the microskills model emphasizes
communication skills and listening. You will find that learning the
specific microskills can be very beneficial in understanding the
thoughts and feelings of students and your colleagues. Then with
that understanding of the other person's frame of reference, you
can better communicate your own ideas.

It is the interchange between listening and influencing, pacing
and leading, that is essential to conflict negotiation and mediation.

Each of the remaining chapters stresses an important communication skill or concept that is critical in effectively communicating
with students or peers. Table 1.1 presents the several skills you will
encounter in this book.

You will find that attending behavior as presented in chapter 2
is a foundation skill for pacing and leading all communication
situations.

Chapter 3 will present questioning skills and how teachers can
use open-ended questions effectively in the classroom. Included

TABLE 1.1 Skills for Pacing and Leading

Skill	Pacing and Leading Function
Attending behavior	Allows you to observe and match the other person's nonverbal and verbal communication style
Questioning	Facilitates understanding of other frames of reference but also gives you control of amount of and direction of talk
Reflecting	Especially useful for pacing and understanding other people's point of view
Structuring	Shows how to plan interpersonal encounters to achieve results, whether a brief chance encounter with one person or a planned meeting with a group
Focusing	Shows how to lead individual and group to a comprehensive understanding of a problem, thus promoting better decisions
Confronting	Shows how to combine pacing and leading in useful ways for negotiation and creative problem solving
Influencing	Requires the ability to communicate interpersonal influence clearly and effectively

will be a discussion of how teachers and administrators can deal with feelings sensitively and soundly.

Chapter 4 will introduce the central skill of active listening—its role in every aspect of the school environment and how it can help shape both the atmosphere and overall tone of the school.

Chapter 5 will discuss focusing as an extension of effective listening. Implicit in the concept is individualizing the curriculum according to the needs of each student.

Chapter 6 will discuss the influencing skills and how the pacing and leading skills of communication can help promote a caring, vital atmosphere in the schools conducive to learning.

Problem-solving skills will be an additional element introduced in chapter 7. Often, good listening skills and strategies for solving problems go hand in hand. There are many opportunities in the school environment for using problem solving—disciplinary actions, planning lessons, curriculum planning sessions, personnel decisions, and working with students who have special needs.

Conflict resolution and presenting alternatives to violence is the topic for chapter 8. Various approaches to conflict resolution such as peer mediation will be presented along with the communication skills pertinent to conflict resolution strategies.

Chapter 9 will discuss how the skills in this book can be effectively applied and used to help create a more sensitive, responsive, and less violent school environment.

Samurai Teaching

Japanese masters of the swords learn their skills through a set of highly detailed training exercises. The process of masterful swordsmanship is broken down into specific skills and studied carefully—one at a time.

Each single skill is practiced until a fine point of mastery is achieved. Perfection and smoothness of execution is the goal. Once the Samurai complete their course of training, they retreat to a mountaintop to meditate and forget about the skills they have just learned. Upon returning to the lowlands, they have naturally integrated the skills into their being.

Excellence in education requires masterful communication: the ability to listen and learn, to focus and confront, and to lead and influence others. Critical to all these skills is mastery in the sense of the Samurai. The skills of this book are easy to understand and—with patience and practice—equally easy to master. But understanding is not mastery. As you know, ideas can be learned today and forgotten tomorrow. This book is concerned with the mastery and application of basic communication skills. Just as mastery for the Samurai required practice of each skill of swordsmanship until learning was honed to a fine point, your mastery level will depend on your interest and your ability to learn each concept well.

Producing this book has taken 30 years of observation in the schools and clinical settings. It is a distillation of a multitude of observations, experiences, and empirical research. However, it can be read in a relatively short time. Its value and lasting potential rely on a relationship of dialogue with you, because it is you and your application of these concepts that will make them live and grow through effective dialogue and communication with others.

References

Aspy, D. N., & Roebuck, F. N. (1977). *Kids don't learn from people they don't like.* Amherst, MA: Human Resource Development Press.

Baker, S., & Daniels, T. (1989). Integrating research on the microcounseling program: A meta-analysis. *Journal of Counseling Psychology, 36,* 213-222.

Daniels, T., & Ivey, A. (in press). *Microcounseling* (3rd edition). Springfield, IL: Charles C Thomas.

Elam, S. M., Rose, L. C., & Gallup, A. M. (1994). The 26th annual Phi Delta Kappa/Gallup poll of the public's attitudes toward the public schools. *Phi Delta Kappan, 76*(1), 41-56.

Himmelfarb, G. (1994-1995). A de-moralized society: The British/American experience. *American Educator, 18*(4), 14-21.

Ivey, A. E. (1974). The clinician as a teacher of interpersonal skills: Let's give away what we've got. *The Clinical Psychologist, 27,* 6-9.

Johnson, J., & Immerwahr, J. (1994-1995). First things first: What Americans expect from the public schools. *American Educator, 18*(4), 4-13.

Kahn, B. B., & Kahn, W. J. (1990). I am the author books. *Elementary School Guidance and Counseling, 25*(2), 153-157.

Kohn, A. (1991). Caring kids: The role of the schools. *Phi Delta Kappan, 72*(7), 496-506.

Kottler, J. A., & Kottler, E. (1993). *Teacher as counselor.* Newbury Park, CA: Corwin.

Morse, P. S. (1994). A survey of college students' reactions to their K-12 teachers and schools. *Education, 115*(1), 133-136.

Morse, P. S., & Brand, L. (1995). *Young children at home and in school: 212 educational activities for their parents, teachers, and caregivers.* Boston: Allyn & Bacon.

Noddings, N. (1995). A morally defensible mission for schools in the 21st century. *Phi Delta Kappan, 76*(5), 365-368.

Pelsma, D. M. (1987). Improving counselor effectiveness: Consulting with style. *School Counselor, 34*(3), 195-201.

Rogers, C. R., & Freiberg, H. J. (1994). *Freedom to learn.* New York: Merrill.

Rosen, C. L. (1982, April 26-30). *Psychotherapeutic techniques application to remedial treatment of reading disabilities.* Paper presented at the 27th annual meeting of the International Reading Association, Chicago.

Rothwell, W. J. (1984). The business writing instructor as counselor. *ABCA Bulletin 47*(3), 49-52.

Spear, K. I. (1978). Psychotherapy and composition. *College Composition and Communication, 29,* 372-374.

Wagner, T. (1995). What's school really for, anyway? And who should decide? *Phi Delta Kappan, 76*(5), 393-399.

2

The Basics of Communication

Communication begins when one person communicates with another. If you have information to pass on to a colleague or a student group, it all begins with the communication of information. But nothing is communicated without listening. And so, the major question in this chapter is What are the foundations of listening and communication?

One of the best ways to understand the ideas of pacing and attending behaviors is to recall what they are not. For example, consider how disturbing it is when you aren't listened to and your message is misunderstood by someone else, or perhaps even ignored.

Take a moment to recall a teacher or perhaps even a family member who failed to listen to you. What did he or she do in failing to listen? How did you feel when you weren't listened to, your message was distorted, or, perhaps even worse, you and your message were ignored?

What Listening Is Not

In most of modern society we are inclined to talk rather than listen. Those who do not listen often need to pace more, "walking with" a person through his or her view of the world. Poor listeners who tend not to take advantage of pacing

1. Often do not look at the other person. By not looking, we frequently communicate rather tangibly that we do not see the person in front of us.

2. Frequently have body posture that indicates that they aren't listening. How many times can you recall someone who failed to pay attention to you whose arms were folded tightly, whose legs were jiggling, or whose body was turned away from you?

3. May be found to have a harsh vocal tone or rapid speech that puts people off. Sometimes a teacher's voice might sound bored, supercilious, disdainful, or uninterested.

4. Tend to take charge of the topic and ignore what others say. Teachers can frequently short-circuit a classroom discussion by beginning to expound at length on a topic, thus interrupting or ceasing the flow and interchange that was taking place in the classroom.

One of the five needs that William Glasser (1986) identifies as basic in all people is the need for power. In the case of students, satisfying their need for power means simply that teachers recognize them, listen to them, and try to give them some say in the classroom. Simply listening to students and trying to pace them will help give them the power they desire, and they will work harder in school as a result (Glasser, 1986, p. 27).

Effective Attending and Pacing

Pacing demands that we be able to listen to other people. If we are to influence or lead them, we must first understand their way of thinking. If the above list reveals what listening is not, then the following provides a helpful summary of what is necessary for effective pacing and listening (Ivey, 1971, 1994):

1. *Eye contact:* Looking at one another as we talk is one of the most effective and direct ways of communicating nonverbally. If you are going to talk to someone, look at him or her, but not for too long, because that can be misconstrued as threatening. Also, looking away too often can be distracting and might convey the message that you are not interested in what the speaker has to say. Not only are the eyes the window of the soul, but they are also the window of our consciousness of other individuals.

2. *Body language:* In Western culture, we communicate our interest via facing the individual squarely and directly or at a 90-degree angle. We lean forward and maintain an open posture, indicative of our interest in listening to the other. By relaxing the muscles of your face, for example, smiling or looking pleasant, you subtly facilitate the other person's relaxing also.

3. *Vocal tone and speech rate:* As we listen to the other, we may find our own vocal tone imitating or harmonizing with the other person. We communicate warmth, interest, and authority through our voice.

4. *Staying on the topic:* The effective listener stays with the other person. In the case of a classroom teacher, simply staying with students and their topics when appropriate will help communicate your attentiveness to their message and frame of reference.

In essence, attending behavior involves a temporary surrender of the self to the other. You show that you want to hear about and understand the other person's point of view, idea, or explanation.

Simply attending to students and listening to them can produce impressive results if a whole school practices these behaviors. For example, at Central Park East Secondary School in East Harlem, New York, each staff member meets with 10-15 students daily for at least 45 minutes. The staff is there for all students, who are free to share everything from academic problems to racism, violence in their lives, and difficult relationships at home. Deborah Meier, the school director, reports that the school has 100% attendance, with 90% graduating. Of those, 95% go on to 4-year colleges—many in the Ivy League.

Multicultural and Personal Implications of Attending

Our country has a growing multicultural population. Although about 22% of the total population are members of minority groups, 30% of school-age children are minority, a figure that will increase to 36% shortly after the year 2000. By the year 2010, the number of minority young people in the U.S. will increase by 4.4 million, while the number of non-Hispanic White young people will decline by 3.8 million (Hodgkinson, 1993, p. 620). Teachers need to be ever more aware of the cultural differences between ethnic groups, particularly the differences in attending skills. Consider Table 2.1. It demonstrates how attending behavior as it is used in middle-class Western culture is not necessarily appropriate with all others (Ivey, Gluckstern, & Ivey, 1993; Ivey, Ivey, & Simek-Morgan, 1993).

TABLE 2.1 Cultural Variations in Attending Behavior

Attending Behavior	*Contrasting Example From Other Cultures*
Eye contact	Many African Americans and people from Spanish-speaking nations and other cultures view avoidance of direct eye contact as a sign of respect.
Body language	People in some African cultures may view direct face-to-face contact as too aggressive. Middle Eastern individuals may have a much closer conversational distance than Europeans.
Vocal tone and speech rate	People in Spanish and Italian groups may talk faster than others. Americans may talk louder whereas British people may unconsciously communicate feelings of superiority.
Adherence to topic	American and German people tend to be direct, whereas people from Japanese and other Asian cultures may be more subtle, not closing a contract until the last moment.

As you review this brief summary of similarities and differences, you may note that each culture has a distinct way of attending. At times, these cultural differences result in misunderstandings and stereotyping such as the "loud Americans," the "arrogant Germans," or the "elusive Japanese." None of the above cultures necessarily possesses these characteristics. What is actually going on in various social situations is our experience of rather different styles of cultural communication. One style is not necessarily "wrong" or "right." However, each style is, of necessity, different from the others, and it is these differences to which we must attend and that we must respect if we are to communicate.

It is especially important for administrators and teachers to listen to and pace students of different cultures through attending skills that help each understand the other.

Individual students can be stereotyped also. Although there are cultural norms, each person within each culture is different. We need to respect individual differences among students. For example, it is inappropriate to maintain eye contact all the time. Naturally varying eye contact is most appropriate, and when we are talking with students of certain cultural backgrounds, it may be best to avoid direct eye contact or to change body posture, vocal tone, or the pattern of attention.

How do you know when to shift your style? Start with attending skills themselves. Observe the reactions of your students to various ways of communicating nonverbally. Then change your communication style to be more in harmony with them.

Mirroring, Pacing, and Leading

The most powerful use of pacing and leading occurs when you mirror the nonverbal behaviors of the person you are trying to understand. You simply assume the body posture of the other person, mirror key movements, and consciously try to use their most important main words.

In mirroring, you seek to become one-in-harmony with the person you are trying to understand. Mirroring may be useful in a situation where your desire is to learn where the other person is "coming from." For example, if you are the principal in an encounter with a teacher where you may be upset over something the teacher did, mirroring the behavior of the other accomplishes three central objectives. First, it enables you to distance yourself temporarily from the heated situation by forcing you to think of the other person rather than becoming embroiled in your own anger or frustration.

Second, deliberate mirroring enables you to better enter the perspective of the other person. While you are calming down, you can gain perspective on the situation and the other person.

Finally, those who mirror each other nonverbally tend to have higher levels of understanding and empathy. When two people are communicating well, their shoulders face each other squarely, they lean slightly toward one another, and their body movements generally mirror each other. On the other hand, if one participant places his or her arms across the chest, crosses the legs away from the other person, or turns the head slightly, there is a good possibility that the person does not agree or feel comfortable with the other person (Thompson & Kleiner, 1992, p. 82).

Attending Skills in the Classroom

Children must learn to become experts at reading body language. In some cases, their very survival depends upon being able to accurately interpret adults' facial expressions, the tension in their muscles, or the way they are carrying themselves. Students are also adept at determining what a teacher's mood is by his or her facial expression, tone of voice, body gestures, and the way he or she approaches the class. The face is the most obvious conveyor of feelings. Some studies indicate that facial expression accounts for about 90% of the communication between two people (Thompson & Kleiner, 1992, p. 82).

Perhaps the best way to discuss good attending behavior in the classroom is to present what often happens in a typical class. Frequently, when a teacher is lecturing, presenting material from an overhead projector, or writing on the board, eye contact with the class is infrequent or entirely absent. That gives students the impression that their presence somehow doesn't count, and they tend to get restless and distracted.

One of the ways of demonstrating that you are attending is by making eye contact with all the students with whom you are interacting. In a full class discussion, try to make gentle eye contact (not a constant stare, but looking and occasionally glancing away) with the student who is speaking while moving toward him or her. And a forward trunk lean can be effected whether you are sitting or standing.

Students respond when you really do try to give them your undivided attention. Different teachers show this in different ways. For example, if you are truly engaged in the dialogue of a class discussion and it is natural for you to pace a little or frown while you are thinking, then do so. It is very difficult not to communicate attention if in fact you are engrossed in the discussion. If you are excited about a point, don't hesitate to show enthusiasm in your voice, even if you start speaking a little louder or faster than normal. Both boredom and excitement are infectious.

Speaking in a natural, confident style, much as you would when speaking to a friend, helps set a subtle but effective tone in the class. In a recent study that examined the use of communication skills when teachers were working with individual students in writing conferences, fully 50% of the teachers in the study demonstrated little or no attending skills when they conferenced with their students. When the teacher didn't use good attending skills, the students soon became restless and stopped paying attention. Sometimes it almost seemed that if a student had gotten up and left the room, the teacher scarcely would have noticed because of the attention being given to the work rather than the person. When teachers affirmed and engaged the students and paid attention to them by making eye contact, leaning over their work, and speaking in a friendly, enthusiastic tone of voice, the students generally stayed on task (Morse, 1994, p. 13).

Teachers who learn to read the nonverbal messages of their class often can avoid discipline problems or students who fail to pay attention. Students frequently are more obvious and expressive than adults when it comes to body language, so the glazed-over look, fidgeting, or the general posture of the class can be indicative of how the class is feeling. Many teachers can tell if most class members are upright and alert or whether there is a general slumping posture in the class. When the latter occurs, some energizing activities like stretching or playing a brief interactive game are appropriate and timely.

Sometimes, but not always, you can tell what children are going through by the expressions on their faces, how they dress, or the way they carry themselves. And at times it is helpful to check with a student to see whether what he is communicating nonverbally is in fact how he is feeling. Simply reading class members' nonverbal communications sensitively can be an important way of sending the message that you care about them. The opposite is also true— not accurately reading body language or checking with a student can lead to more isolation, agitation, and potential classroom disruption.

Five guidelines are generally helpful in responding effectively to nonverbal communication. They include (a) making a conscious effort to focus your attention on the cues that seem to pertain at that moment, (b) seeing each of the nonverbal messages in the proper context, (c) noting incongruities as they come up, (d) heightening your own awareness of how you feel about the particular interaction in question, and (e) reflecting your understandings of the nonverbal messages back to the sender for his or her confirmation or correction (Bolton, 1986, p. 88).

Exercises in Attending Behavior

1. From time to time, scan the class to see what the overall body postures of your students seem to be. Are most members of the class alert, attentive, or generally slumping in their seats or sitting listlessly?

2. Make frequent eye contact and try to determine what the students' eyes seem to be communicating. Do you see excitement, trust, boredom, anger, sadness, happiness?

3. Listen to your students' tone of voice. See if you can determine the mood from the tone. For example, a monotone is often a sign of boredom, a tense or loud tone might be one of anger, and a slow or low pitch could be an indication of depression.

4. If you are trying to communicate with a student and some nonverbal communication seems discrepant, check with the sender to see if you are reading him or her correctly.

5. The next time you have a conference with one student or a small group, deliberately engage in nonattending behavior. For example, when a student starts talking to you, deliberately avoid eye

contact, use poor or closed body posture, and change topics frequently. Then, switch your style and start listening, using good attending skills. Note the difference.

6. Take a student with whom you are having problems aside and try pacing him or her by deliberately engaging in good attending behavior. See what you can learn from the encounter. Particularly important in this phase is letting the student temporarily take charge of the topic to be discussed. While using attending behavior in this leading fashion, maintain relaxed eye contact, open body language, and an easy, relaxed vocal tone.

7. Deliberately mirror the nonverbal behaviors of other people. It is usually best to start with a good friend, colleague, or even a family member. Engage in conversation and use good attending skills to draw out the friend or associate. Once this person is talking smoothly, deliberately mirror his or her body posture and gestures. You will find that it takes practice to do so smoothly.

References

Bolton, R. (1986). *People skills.* New York: Simon & Schuster.

Glasser, W. (1986). *Control theory in the classroom.* New York: Harper & Row.

Hodgkinson, H. (1993). American education: The good, the bad, and the task. *Phi Delta Kappan, 74*(8), 619-625.

Ivey, A. (1971). *Microcounseling: Innovations in interviewing.* Springfield, IL: Charles C Thomas.

Ivey, A. (1994). *Intentional interviewing and counseling: Facilitating development in a multicultural society.* Pacific Grove, CA: Brooks/Cole.

Ivey, A., Gluckstern, N., & Ivey, M. (1993). *Basic attending skills videotapes* (3rd ed.). North Amherst, MA: Microtraining.

Ivey, A., Ivey, M., & Simek-Morgan, L. (1993). *Counseling and psychotherapy: A multicultural perspective* (3rd ed.). Boston: Allyn & Bacon.

Morse, P. S. (1994). The writing teacher as helping agent: Communicating effectively in the conferencing process. *Journal of Classroom Interaction, 29*(1), 9-15.

Thompson, P. A., & Kleiner, B. H. (1992, September) How to read nonverbal communication. *The Bulletin,* 81-83.

3

Questioning Skills
and Effective Teaching

Socrates is considered one of the best questioners in the history of humankind. His questioning style was designed to draw out knowledge that was thought to be existent in the other person. In his famous dialogue with the slave boy, Socrates sets out to prove that the youth has the inherent knowledge of a complex geometrical theory.

But did Socrates draw out information from the slave boy or did he simply impart his own knowledge through systematic questioning? Consider the following selections:

Socrates: Is this a four-cornered space having all these lines equal, all four?

Boy: Surely.

Socrates: And these across the middle, are they not equal too?

Boy: Yes——

Socrates: Are not these four lines equal, and don't they contain this space within them?

Boy: Yes, that is right.

Socrates: Just consider: How big is this space?

Boy: I don't understand.

Socrates: Does not each of these lines cut each of these spaces, four spaces in half? Is that right?

Boy: Yes.

Socrates: How many spaces as big as that are in this middle space?

Boy: Four.

Socrates: How many in this one (A)?

Boy: Two.

Socrates: How many times two is four?

Boy: Twice.

Socrates: Then, how many (square) feet big is this middle space?

Boy: Eight (square) feet.

(Plato's *Meno in Rouse*, 1956, pp. 43-49)

Socrates, Closed Questions, and Leading the Witness

Did the slave boy have the knowledge, or was it Socrates's leading questions that led to the resolution of the mathematical question?

When you ask questions using Socrates' style, do you gain any new information?

If you use leading questions well, you can put your ideas in the other person's mind very effectively. All it takes is your leading the witness with a chain of reasoning to support your own conclusions.

Clearly asking questions is a good way to lead others. We can do well to be like Socrates or a skilled lawyer so we can quickly and efficiently get at the facts we need. Through structured and closed questions we can save time and get our ideas across.

Closed questions tend to be leading questions that can be answered with a few words. Often these questions can be answered with a "yes" or "no." With closed questions, there tends to be a right and wrong answer—and the person who determines correctness is the questioner.

Like Socrates, a skilled lawyer in a court trial wants the witness to come up with the prescribed, prepared answer. Effective use of closed questions ensures that the lead and control remain in the hands of the inquirer and that no new data cloud the situation.

The problem, of course, with Socrates and the legal closed-question approach is that the answer is already known. All that is needed is a parrot to feed back ready-made answers to the questioner.

There are plenty of questions in Socrates's dialogue above, but did they really help the slave boy become a more confident and independent thinker? Some teachers also ask lots of questions but, as with Socrates, the answers to the questions are merely part of a recitation approach—the teacher already knows the answers and simply uses "canned questions" as a way of leading the students to the preconceived points in the lesson plans. The end result is the appearance of class participation, but in reality the students are passive agents in the process and are marginally involved, at best. As with the slave boy-Socrates dialogue, the teacher does the thinking, calls the shots, and otherwise controls the overall learning event.

The following is an example from a kindergarten classroom of the kind of questioning we often see in classrooms when "recitation questions" are employed:

Teacher: Now, I have a letter that's up here on the bulletin board. Could someone tell me what that letter is?

Student: "S."

Teacher: Yes. Did you ever hear it in mother's kitchen? Where have you heard it in mother's kitchen?

Student: When my mother's cooking and it gets too hot and it goes "ssss."

Teacher: What is she usually cooking when it does that?

Student: No, my father's always cooking it —deer meat.

Teacher: Oh, deer meat. Does he cook it in a pan?

Student: He fries deer meat.

Teacher: That's the thing—when they fry it! Then you hear "ssss." Do you have bicycles? When do you hear "S" around a bicycle?

Student: When you ride on a wet road.

Teacher: No, it comes from something round and when you press it down air escapes from it.

Student: The wheel.

Teacher: Not the wheel, the what?

Student: The tire.

Teacher: Yes, the tire!

(CBS News, 1972, *What's New at School*)

The students quickly learn that they are to feed into what the teacher is looking for and any answer other than hers is not the correct one.

But it is their curiosity, their innate joy in discovering the world and reveling in the "sense of wonder" about life, not passivity, that will help students become intelligent, discerning, thinking citizens. Students need to engage in the discussion of controversial matters and learn how to make responsible decisions both for themselves and for others. And that all comes from the ability to develop and sustain a substantive atmosphere of questioning in the classroom.

Unfortunately, much classroom discourse rules out student questions. Besides using questions as part of recitations, the nature of many textbooks and workbooks discourages active questioning, as does the often-relentless need to cover ground in the subject area. For example, reading skills, mathematics, and history all require the coverage of considerable amounts of material, and as a result student questions often are put on the back burner.

What further discourages questions in the classroom is that it is often not considered "cool" to display interest in the subject matter or to carry on a healthy dialogue with the teacher. Intellectual curiosity is simply not "with-it" behavior in many classrooms.

Making Questions Work for Both You and Others

Developing a healthy questioning attitude is the basis for many of the higher-order thinking skills and intellectual values that encourage students to question what is presented to them for its truth and validity. Being encouraged to ask questions develops an independence of thought and an overall curiosity that can only come when a learner feels that his or her questions are valued and taken seriously.

Thinking requires a certain intellectual ferment, a struggle with something that interests and excites the individual. In contrast to closed questions, open-ended questions invite maximal room for thought and involvement in the overall classroom discourse.

Open questions often begin with what, how, could or would, or why. Questions beginning with "what" lead to factual information and encourage a child to talk about the key facts or details of a situation ("What happened when you saw your cat was frightened by a truck?"). "How" questions most often help a child talk about process, sequence, and emotions ("How did you feel when you heard about that?"). Questions that begin with "could" or "would" tend to provide the maximum amount of room for a response ("Could you tell me more about your visit?").

Research reveals that "could" questions put focus on the student in a comfortable way and seem to establish trust. Technically, "could" questions can be answered with a "yes" or "no," but relatively few students stop there. "Could" questions seem to empower the student to answer questions as he or she wishes.

"Why" questions typically ask people to search for reasons undergirding their behavior, thoughts, or emotions. "Why" questions and their search for reasons often, but not always, seem to put people on the spot. These questions are sometimes difficult to answer because we don't always know why we or others do things. For example, if you ask a child who is drawing a picture, "Why didn't you include the color of your car?" it might be impossible to answer, and it also could make the student feel that she or he has done something wrong in some vague, ill-defined way. "What," "how," and "could" questions provide more room, and providing space for growth is one basic dimension of being an effective helper.

On the other hand, some "why" questions can be most useful in the classroom or in complex two-person communication. First, before using "why," you should ask, Is there sufficient trust to allow mutual exploration? Although "why" questions do tend to put people on the spot, if you work together to explore the reasons and wherefores of an action or an issue, "why" can be helpful.

Some possibly contextually useful "why" questions include the following.

1. (Asked with an open frame of mind) "Sue, why do you think that the conflict with Sam occurred? Let me listen to your ideas for a while."

2. "Class, why do you think the native American Indian nations are unhappy with the way U.S. history is written? Share your ideas."
3. "Oscar, why do girls object to your saying things in a sexist manner?"
4. "Mrs. Jones, why do you imagine that your son's teacher might organize her class that way?"

Emotions Are Important in the Classroom

Although much of the discussion in this chapter is directed toward the use of questions in classroom instruction, questions can also help you to handle emotions—which is also an inevitable part of both a teacher's and an administrator's job. Emotions, many times, lead our actions. Feelings and emotions represent value statements of your colleagues and students. The importance a teacher or student applies to a problem is often predicated on his or her feeling or emotional level. Dealing with the emotions of an upset student or a teacher can do much to help either party calm down enough to get back to the task at hand. When you ask well-placed and sensitive questions that deal with the person's emotions ("How does that make you feel?" or "What did you feel when he said that?"), you can also reflect feelings, as outlined in chapter 4.

Encouraging Student Questions

Fortunately, there are ways of encouraging student questions. When a student asks a question, listen and attend to it with sensitivity and caring (see chapter 4). Try to appreciate why a student is asking the question or, if you ask a question, what led him or her to give a particular answer. Giving students your undivided attention when they do ask a question communicates that you value the active exploration of areas of concern and interest to the student.

Sometimes students don't know what they really want to ask, and you can help clarify what is on their mind. After listening reflectively, you can sometimes rephrase or reframe the question to see if that was what they had in mind. And asking questions such as "Have I missed anything?" or "What would you add to what I just said?" helps open the discussion to mutuality.

Simply waiting patiently for student questions or allowing time for students to ask questions is often very productive. Thanking them for asking a question is also an effective encouragement.

Similarly, waiting after asking a well-phrased question is an equally good strategy. The average time teachers usually wait in allowing a student to answer a question before rephrasing it, calling on someone else, or answering it themselves is less than 1 second. However, studies show that when wait time is increased to 3 to 5 seconds, good things happen: Students participate more actively in the class by asking more questions and answering the questions more fully. Also, there is an increase in student-initiated responses and overall class interaction among students.

Another idea is to have students ask each other questions based on what another student has just said. That can include you, the teacher. Research shows that student responses to student questions often are longer and more substantive than answers to teacher questions.

Sustaining students' questions by mulling them over and including them in a class discussion is another way of encouraging them. You are validating their questions by including them in the general dialogue of the class. Also, simply saying "That's a good question" or "That really gives us something to think about" is a way of positively acknowledging the student's contribution. In addition, coming back to student questions later ("Let's discuss for a moment the question that _____ asked a minute ago") is a way of demonstrating that you welcome their questions and take them seriously.

At various times during the class you can encourage students to volunteer questions for discussion. You can also ask them to make up questions for study guides or even tests. Writing out such questions is a good integrated activity with the teaching of writing. Not only does it help sharpen a student's thinking about a particular point or concept, but it also helps in the writing process.

Questions and Higher-Order Thinking Skills

In encouraging higher-order thinking skills through mostly open-ended questions, the following taxonomy of generic questions (Paul, 1993, pp. 341-344) can help teachers create a classroom where a sense of lively inquiry and in-depth thinking is the norm:

Questions of Clarification

- What do you mean by ____?
- What is your main point?
- How does ____ relate to ____?
- Could you put that another way?
- Is your basic point ____ or ____?
- What do you think is the main issue here?
- Let me see if I understand you; do you mean ____ or ____?
- How does this relate to our discussion (problem, issue)?
- What do you think (John) meant by his remark? What did you take (John) to mean?
- (Jane), would you summarize in your own words what (Richard) has said?—(Richard), is that what you meant?
- Could you give me an example?
- Would this be an example: ____?
- Could you explain that further?
- Would you say more about that?
- Why do you say that?

Questions That Probe Assumptions

- What are you assuming?
- What is (Karen) assuming?
- What could we assume instead?
- You seem to be assuming ____? Do I understand you correctly?
- All of your reasoning depends on the idea that ____. Why have you based your reasoning on ____ rather than ____?
- You seem to be assuming ____. How would you justify taking this for granted?
- Is it always the case? Why do you think the assumption holds here?
- Why would someone make this assumption?

Questions That Probe Reasons and Evidence

- What would be an example?
- How do you know?
- Why do you think that is true?
- Do you have any evidence for that?
- What difference does that make?
- What are your reasons for saying that?
- What other information do we need?
- Could you explain your reasons to us?
- But is that good evidence to believe that?
- Is there reason to doubt that evidence?
- Who is in a position to know if that is so?
- What would you say to someone who said ____?
- Can someone else give evidence to support that response?
- By what reasoning did you come to that conclusion?
- How could we find out whether that is true?
- Are these reasons adequate?
- Why did you say that?
- What led you to that belief?
- How does that apply to this case?
- What would change your mind?

Questions About Viewpoints or Perspectives

- You seem to be approaching this issue from ____ perspective. Why have you chosen this rather than that perspective?
- How would other groups or types of people respond? Why? What would influence them?
- How could you answer the objection that ____ would make?
- What might someone who believed ____ think?
- Can/does anyone see this another way?
- What would someone who disagrees say?
- What is an alternative?
- How are (Ken's) and (Roxanne's) ideas alike? Different?

Questions That Probe Implications and Consequences

- What are you implying by that?
- When you say ____, are you implying ____?
- But if that happened, what else would happen as a result? Why?

- What effect would that have?
- Would that necessarily happen or only probably happen?
- What is an alternative?
- If this and this are the case, then what else must also be true?
- If we say that this is unethical, how about that?

Questions About the Question

- How can we find out?
- What does this question assume?
- Would ____ put the question differently?
- Why is this question important?
- How could someone settle this question?
- Can we break this question down at all?
- Is the question clear? Do we understand it?
- Is this question easy or hard to answer? Why?
- Does this question ask us to evaluate something?
- Do we all agree that this is the question?
- To answer this question, what questions would we have to answer first?
- I'm not sure I understand how you are interpreting the main question at issue.
- Is this the same issue as ____?
- How would ____ put the issue?

Exercises in Questioning Skills

Understanding the concept of open and closed questions and the possibilities inherent in each will become most beneficial when you take these ideas and use them in positive situations.

The following summary may be useful to you in these exercises:

- Closed questions: Usually begin with "is," "are," or "do," and require a specific answer, often short, with a "yes" or "no" response.
- Open questions: Provide an opportunity for the other person to respond so that you can learn their ideas and frame of reference.

Some key open questions are:

- "What" questions tend to lead to factual information ("What is the capital of Kansas?").
- "How" questions tend to lead to discussion of feelings ("How do you feel about that?").
- "Could" questions tend to be maximally open ("Could you tell me about the situation in your own words?" or "Could you tell me more?").
- "Why" questions tend to lead to discussion of reasons, causation, and past history ("Why do you think Roosevelt said what he did?").

1. Select a friend, colleague, or family member and use the varying question stems above one at a time. Try a string of closed questions and note the result you achieve. Follow this by several "what" questions and see if you tend to bring out facts. Examine the effectiveness of "How do you feel?" Does this draw out feelings and emotions that help you understand the underlying value structure and emotions the person feels toward the issue? Also observe what happens when you use "why" questions. Does this type of question result in defensiveness or hesitation on the part of the person?

2. Tape record a class session in order to see what kinds of questions the students are asking. Also, the same exercise can be useful for you. As a teacher, you may find you are missing some areas. As an administrator, you may find the exercise helpful for becoming more aware of your style.

3. Listen carefully to a student's, or colleague's, or parent's question. Make sure you understand what it is, and then thank him or her for asking it.

4. If your students don't seem to be asking many questions, have a classroom session where your students brainstorm about the reasons why they don't. List all the reasons on the board and ask them to comment on them.

5. Ask students to write out some questions as part of a study guide you may be preparing for the class. You may even consider asking the students for sample test questions.

6. When a student asks a question, ponder it, play with it a bit, and perhaps ask the class what they think of the question. It will demonstrate your interest in the question and will promote class involvement.

7. Carefully write out any questions ahead of time, revising them until you feel they express what you are trying to ask. Try to anticipate what the answers to the questions and your responses to them might be. That may help you devise a sequence of questions that you can use in pursuing a line of inquiry.

8. Rehearse out loud the asking of any questions ahead of time. Think in terms of a desirable wait time, which is usually about 3 to 5 seconds.

9. Ask students to pose questions for discussion and then pick one or two that you feel might yield some good results.

References

CBS News. (1972). *What's new at school.*

Paul, R. (1993). *Critical thinking: How to prepare students for a rapidly changing world.* Santa Rosa, CA: The Foundation for Critical Thinking.

4

Reflecting and the
Basic Listening Sequence:
Entering the World of the Other

When you think back to those teachers who made a particularly positive impression on you, what characteristics come to mind? When we ask that question informally, we find that almost always people cite teachers who considered their feelings and interests, who conveyed a sense of caring, and who seemed to listen to them as the ones they remembered most positively.

The importance of listening extends far beyond its value in helping determine what people are trying to say. The act of listening, in itself, pays others the highest form of compliment. One is saying in effect, "You are important to me and what you are saying really counts."

Simply listening to students and communicating this message has a powerful effect on their self-concept and their ability to learn. Studies have shown that teachers who are empathetic tend to produce higher-achieving students than those with low levels of this quality. It is the most effective way we know to improve the quality of communication with others and one's relationships with them.

This chapter outlines four key skills of reflective listening: encouraging, paraphrasing, reflecting feelings, and summarizing. Coupled with effective questioning, these skills provide you with a systematic checklist to ensure that you have heard and reflected on what other people say. This is basic to creating helping relationships.

Encouraging

People talk and share their ideas when they are encouraged. There are a number of basic responses or minimal "encourages" that can help a student to continue talking (Gordon, 1974, pp. 61-62).

1. *Silence*. Saying nothing at all is a powerful, nonverbal message advocated by William Glasser and other helping agents to convey genuine acceptance and encouragement. Saying nothing but being attentive and interested suggests that you are listening and that you want the person to say more.

2. *Acknowledgment responses*. Often referred to as "empathic grunting," acknowledgment responses use verbal cues like "Uh-huh," "Oh," and "I see," and often include a variety of nonverbal body postures or gestures that let the student know that you are listening. For example, nodding, leaning forward, smiling, frowning, and other body movements, used appropriately, let the student know that you are really listening.

3. *Door openers*. These consist of a few words or short sentences from a student's conversation that pick up on what the student said and encourage him or her to continue. Examples include "Tell me more," "How did you feel about that?" "Give me an example," and "That's something I'd like to hear more about."

Another type of encourage is restatement, the direct repetition of the exact main word or words of the person to whom you are listening. For example, if a student was trying to tell you about his experiences on a roller coaster ride, the conversation might go something like this:

Student: "When we began shooting down the side it was really something else."

Teacher: "Something else?"

Student "Yeah, I could hardly breathe."
Teacher: "Couldn't breathe at all, huh?"
Student: "It was as if everything stopped and we just hung there."

It seems so simple that the power of restatement is easily ignored, and yet research has revealed it to be central to effective communication, and it is used more and more by effective professionals and nonprofessionals.

Although the restatement encourage is clearly a pacing skill because it starts with the exact main words of the other, it is also a powerful leading skill because it almost literally forces the person with whom you are talking to explain in more detail what he or she is discussing. It also helps the person elaborate from his or her own perspective, with minimal influence on your part.

Students want to be recognized on a regular basis and tell you what is on their minds. If you mirror back their important key words in a supportive, questioning tone of voice, you can obtain a lot of information with a minimum effort. Parents of young children can often use this technique fruitfully, especially if they are a bit tired and don't have the time and energy to engage in a full-blown conversation.

Paraphrasing

Minimal encourages demonstrate that one is listening sympathetically and prompt the other person to continue the conversation. Paraphrasing is equally important as a way of showing that you, the teacher, are in fact paying attention and accurately comprehending what the student has to say. Paraphrasing is considered by many helping agents to be the key tool in responding effectively to people. It involves the teacher feeding back to the student the essence of what the teacher thinks the student just said. The teacher does not repeat the student's exact utterance word for word, but rather reflects back what the teacher believes the essence of the message to be.

Go into any elementary classroom where the teacher is noted as particularly effective and you'll almost always find him or her constantly encouraging, restating, and paraphrasing the students' words. Similarly, effective junior and senior high teachers show their students respect by using the same skills.

The following is an example of paraphrasing.

Teacher: "So, what kind of progress are you making on your paper?"

Student: "I just don't like the way it's coming out. I can't seem to think of any ideas."

Teacher: "The paper really has you stumped right now."

The teacher's response does two things: (1) It shows the student that the teacher is listening, and (2) it encourages the student to continue by either picking up on and continuing the idea of the teacher's paraphrase if it is accurate, or clarifying what he or she really wants to say if it is not. For example, if the teacher's paraphrase in the above example is not quite accurate, the student could say: "Well, I'm actually kind of bored with the paper right now and would like to work on it later."

Many teachers who initially begin trying to paraphrase worry about what they are going to say and whether their response is "correct." It is worth noting that for any given message there are dozens of different ways a good listener can respond. It is best not to fret about the perfect response but rather to respond naturally to whatever the student has said. A teacher need only stay with what the student seems to be saying and "give back" to the student what the teacher thinks he or she is trying to express.

Because complete objectivity and comprehensiveness in one's response is a difficult, if not impossible, goal, teachers can learn to make their inevitable selective focusing work for them: They can concentrate on those parts of the conversation that they believe will most help their students and mirror back those elements. The result, while still employing active listening, enables the teacher to respond to those elements of the student's message that come closest to what the teacher perceives as a solution to the task at hand.

For example, if the student seems to be having difficulties with organization in his or her writing, a teacher might try to relate the student's utterances to an examination of a logical flow of ideas.

Such selectivity remains a delicate balancing act between what a student would like to discuss and what the teacher thinks the student needs. The danger, of course, is that the teacher might "take over" and not truly hear what the student wants to talk about. When in doubt, it is usually best to go with as many of the student's concerns as possible. Most students will make the greatest progress if the teacher attends to where they are at the present time. It may be frustrating not to "correct" the obvious problem, but students are notoriously hard of hearing if teachers address their own rather than the students' problems about their writing. Witness the number of times English teachers correct the same misspellings on the same students' papers. The profession has conclusively established that telling students is not enough.

Listening actively can be a very useful skill in many school situations—classroom discussions, handling resistance to learning, helping dependent students, and parent-teacher conferences (Gordon, 1974; Ivey, 1971, 1994). In each case it can help students be more open and honest and encourage them to delve into related areas or expand on existing ones.

Learning to listen to others sympathetically also develops a person's ability to be empathetic to others' points of view, which is an important thinking skill if we want to be fair to ideas that may be alien to us. Giving a fair hearing to an opposing argument is part of the intellectual integrity that defines a good thinker. For example, a well-known peace demonstrator, when confronted with opposition, often walked up to the angry hecklers and asked them what they thought of the demonstration and then listened carefully to their grievances. The heckling invariably stopped, and when the hecklers finished speaking, they often were ready to listen to what the demonstrator had to say.

The following is an example of some active listening done with a fifth-grade student where the teacher and he were going over a paper he had written about a member of his family:

Teacher: So your mom speaks Spanish?

Student: Yeah, she speaks Spanish to everyone in the family and I try to also.

Teacher: So you like to be able to speak like her.

Student: Yes, but she speaks English to some of her friends.

Teacher: Maybe she feels more comfortable doing that?

Student: Yeah. Her friends wouldn't understand her if she spoke just Spanish.

Teacher: It looks as if she speaks a different language to different people, just so she can communicate with them?

Student: That's about it.

Finally, the following questions can help one listen actively.

- Am I able, and do I care enough, to give the student my full attention?
- Do I really prefer talking to listening?
- Am I thinking about the effect I am having on the student?
- What sort of signs and clues am I giving physically and verbally?
- Do I hear what I expect or want to hear?
- Do I listen for hidden messages, both in what is said and how it is said?
- Am I distinguishing between what the student says is the problem and what the real problem is? (Faraday & Harris, 1994)

Reflecting Feelings: Pacing Emotion in the Classroom

The desire for close relationships is universal among children and adults alike. Teachers, are, by definition, in a helping profession, and one cannot separate the emotional from the intellectual components in the teacher-student relationship, especially among students who have not yet matured developmentally. The title of a well-known book written by David Aspy and Flora Roebuck (1977), *Kids Don't Learn From People They Don't Like,* says it all.

In addition, students inevitably bring their troubles to school with them, and sometimes the teacher may be the only stable, secure adult in their lives at that point in time. Having a caring teacher who is willing to talk with a student can do much to help calm the student and bring him or her back into focus. One single teacher who is truly understanding, who takes the trouble to listen to a student, can literally change that student's whole outlook on life.

Many students' responses come from feelings that reflect or relate to something that happened or might happen in their lives. Not only can a teacher help a student sort out facts from emotions, but helping to identify emotions is, once again, a way of showing a student that you are listening. In short, reflection of feelings involves a paraphrasing of a person's emotional state.

The key to reflecting feelings skillfully is the acknowledgment of feelings. Acknowledging feelings is a good place to start practicing with reflecting feelings because it paces the other person's emotional state but does not get you overly involved, and it does not open the other person to extensive evaluation of his or her psyche.

Acknowledgment of feelings focuses on labeling the feeling and feeding it back to the other in terms of a brief emotional paraphrase. If you want acknowledgment to stop there, break eye contact momentarily or perhaps place your hand out, palm down. You will find that acknowledging feeling often puts emotion in its place and under control.

If you decide it is useful to open up emotion and involve oneself in a deeper reflection of feeling, do the same thing, but maintain direct eye contact and good attending behavior, and indicate your acceptance of and interest in hearing more.

In reflecting feelings, the following steps are often the most helpful:

1. Use the student's name from time to time or use the pronoun "you."
2. The feelings must be labeled as specifically and vividly as possible. Give special attention to mixed or ambivalent feelings.
3. Use sentence stems such as "You feel _____ because _____," "You seem to feel _____," "Sounds as if you feel _____," "John (or any name), I sense you're _____," and add the labeled emotion.

4. The context may be paraphrased for additional clarification: "You seem to feel _____ when _____."
5. Reflection of feelings is most often useful if immediate here-and-now feelings are labeled and worked through.

The following excerpt is an example of a teacher concentrating on a student's emotional content.

Student: "I'm going to spend the whole summer with my grand-parents in Georgia!"

Teacher: "You seem to feel pretty excited about staying with them for the summer."

Student: "Yeh, I sort of am but I'm wondering whether there will be anyone my age down there."

Teacher: "You're happy about going but you might also be feeling a little anxious about not having anyone to play with."

Student: "I don't want to be by myself all summer."

Teacher: "Sounds as if you will feel lonely if no one is around."

Remember that acknowledging and reflecting feelings is also a powerful way to accentuate the positive atmosphere of a classroom. For example, simply acknowledging a student's evident happiness in solving a problem or responding well in class ("Carol, you must feel really proud of that paper") can further reinforce his or her good feelings.

Summarizing: Putting Your Pacing Together in an Organized Fashion

A summary is very similar to a paraphrase, but with two major differences. First, the summary covers a longer period of time and is a direct attempt to summarize the main ideas of the other person, and second, the summary is designed as punctuation. It says to the other person, "I hear what you are saying and you seem to be saying the following: _____."

Thus, although the summary is clearly a mode of pacing the other person and indicating that you have heard what is said, it is also a good way to lead a discussion and ensure that needless repetition does not occur.

For example, if a student begins repeating herself endlessly, summarization is a way of simultaneously showing respect for and interest in what she is saying and also bringing the discussion back on track.

Often, at the end of a conference or a class discussion, a teacher needs to help a student pull together what took place and restate or recapitulate the substance of the session. Not only does this put closure on what happened, but it grounds the student and helps him think of the next step he could or should take. Seeing the wider picture not only reinforces for the student what he has accomplished, but also enables him to draw conclusions, sort out his reactions, and see where he's been and where he might be going.

A teacher can use summarization to

1. Begin a class or a conference with an individual student ("I would like to discuss _____," or "In our last meeting we talked about _____")
2. Clarify what is happening as the class or conference proceeds ("Could we stop for a moment and see what has been said so far?")
3. Provide a transition from topic to topic ("So far you've been talking about _____; now _____")
4. Summarize what has transpired over the entire individual conference or class ("Today we talked about _____")

Thus the summary is a reflecting skill that permits both pacing and leading. It is a highly useful way to add control and structure to complex class discussions or individual conferencing sessions with students.

The Basic Listening Sequence

Pacing the other person and entering their frame of reference can be facilitated by using the basic listening sequence (BLS) (Ivey, 1994; Ivey, Gluckstern, & Ivey, 1993). The BLS organizes the skills of the first chapters of this book and leads to concrete results in understanding. The BLS can be used in class discussions or with individuals.

It could be stated that you have three objectives in pacing and reflecting. You seek to understand (a) the key facts of a situation or problem, (b) the important feelings and values related to that situation or problem, and (c) how the other person organizes the facts and feelings. If you can pace and obtain the key facts, feelings, and organization of a problem or situation, you are well prepared to move to a leading posture and problem resolution.

The basic listening sequence may be described as follows.

1. Open questions to obtain a general picture of a problem (including "what" questions to bring out facts and "how" questions to draw out feelings and values about those facts)
2. Encourages to obtain elaboration of the other person's or group's key words, thus leading to more complex factual or personal information
3. Paraphrases to feed back key facts to the individual to make sure that you have heard things accurately
4. Reflections and acknowledgments of feelings to ensure that you have noted key emotions
5. Summaries to organize facts and feelings in a systematic fashion

Table 4.1 illustrates how the BLS could be useful either in an individual conference with a student or in a class situation.

You will find that the basic listening sequence is an invaluable tool in working with both individuals and groups. It enables you to pace the thinking of the other person and helps students and colleagues feel that their needs and ideas have been heard. Finally, this reflective pacing will help you organize your understanding of how others think, thus putting you in a most effective position for leading and influencing the way both individual conferences and the classroom or group proceeds.

The following shows how open questions, encourages, paraphrases, reflections of feelings, and summaries can be combined in

TABLE 4.1 Using the Basic Listening Sequence (BLS) With an Individual or With Your Class

Skill	Using the Skills One-on-One	Using the Skills With the Whole Class
Open question	"Could you explain more about your problem with discipline in your class?"	"What are the chief reasons for England's policy of appeasement?"
Encourage (Exact words of other person)	"Chaos?" or "The boys won't pay attention?"	"The threat of bombing?" "Chamberlain was being nice?"
Paraphrase	"Sounds as if the trouble occurs mostly after lunch."	"As I hear it you feel that England should not have negotiated."
Reflection of Feelings	"You're pretty miserable with the way the class is going."	"So, the class generally seems to be upset with England's actions."
Summary	"So, it seems that the discipline issues occur mainly after lunch when the boys are especially active on the playing field. It makes you pretty frustrated. Have I heard the situation correctly?"	"To summarize where we are right now, most of you seem to feel England gave away too much to Germany and that they should have paid more attention to the cities. Let's see if that helps explain why England was bombed."

an interaction between a first grader and her teacher in preparation for a writing assignment.

Teacher: Could you tell me about the five nice things that happened to you?

Student: I had a cat named Smokey and she is still with us.

Teacher: I see. Is there anything else?

Student: I had him when we moved into another house.

Teacher: So you moved to another house just recently, right?

Student: That's why I'm at this school.

Teacher: What other nice things can you write about?

Student: About me and my brother.

Teacher: O.K. What made that nice for you?

Student: Because me and him went to the park with my dad.

Teacher: Went to the park with your dad. I'll bet that was fun. You and your brother.

Student: Um.

Teacher: And would you like to tell about the fish?

Student: We caught the fish in the creek. We caught one that big and it was real green and it had a big mouth.

Teacher: Green. What kind of fish was it?

Student: It's a carp.

Teacher: You caught a carp? O.K.

Student: And then we ate some cake.

Teacher: When did you eat some cake?

Student: Recently.

Teacher: Recently?

Student: It was a strawberry cake.

Teacher: Yum! You know how I am about food. You'll be able to share some really nice things this afternoon—you talked about your cat, your trip to the park with your brother and your dad, about the fish you caught, and the yummy cake you ate. See if you can write down some of what you just told me before we meet this afternoon.

Exercises in Reflective Listening

1. Talk with a colleague or a student about something you know is of real interest to him or her. Listen carefully to key words used by this individual. Repeat these words back with a questioning

tone of voice. Note other main words and repeat them back. You will find that you have a powerful tool for directing conversational flow and obtaining a more in-depth understanding of how other people come to their unique perceptions and views of problems and situations. Increasingly, this simple but profound skill is seen as basic to true communication and understanding.

2. Ask triads of students to take turns sharing "one of the most exciting things you have ever done." The listener listens actively, reflecting and responding to what is said. The observer checks to see how well the listener is listening (whether he is interrupting, looking at the speaker, paying attention, etc.). Each person gets a chance to be a speaker, listener, and observer.

3. Try this out the next time you or your class gets into a spirited class discussion or argument. Stop the discussion and institute the following rule: Allow each person to speak only after he or she has restated the ideas and feelings of the previous speaker accurately and to that person's satisfaction. It may slow down the class temporarily, but it will dramatize the importance of listening accurately to other people and what happens when you don't.

4. Teachers and administrators are often leery of working with students' emotions. Thus the brief acknowledgment of feeling is often a better place to start than the full-blown reflection of feeling.

For a trial run, try one of the following acknowledgments of feelings with a busy server in a restaurant:

"Looks as if you're pretty hassled right now."
"I can see you're feeling tired with all this rush."

Or, after observing an angry exchange with a nearby table:

"Having someone like that to wait on must be pretty frustrating."

5. You can then try acknowledgments of feelings with a colleague in a faculty room interaction or with a student who comes up to you after class and shares with you something that is on his or her mind.

6. The next time you have a class discussion, take a minute to summarize what seems to have been said. Then ask a few members of the class whether they feel you have left anything out. Often, that will stimulate further discussion or will let a student include something that he or she didn't get a chance to say during the discussion.

7. Ask a few friends or colleagues to play the role of two agitated parents who are engaged in a parent conference with you. See if you can apply the communication skills of attending, questioning, encouraging, active listening, summarizing, and reflecting feelings.

8. The basic listening sequence brings together all the pacing skills of this book in a useful and systematic framework. It is not necessary to follow the exact sequence. The BLS is oriented to results, and your effectiveness with it can be measured by asking yourself whether or not you (a) obtain the key facts, (b) learn how the other person feels about those facts, and (c) know how the facts and feelings are organized.

When you practice the BLS, start with a willing family member or colleague. Select a topic of mutual interest. Perhaps even with the book in your hand, try the following:

a. Open question: "Could you tell me about _____?"
b. Follow up with open questions beginning with "what" and "how" to get more information. Use closed questions to obtain needed specific data.
c. Note important key words used by the other person. Repeat them back, using the other person's exact words.
d. Paraphrase back to the person what has been said to you. Use the other person's main words, but keep it just a bit briefer.
e. Acknowledge feelings. Search out how the other person values or feels about that topic. "You feel _____ about _____."
f. Summarize what the person has been saying and ask him or her, "Have I heard you correctly?" Aim to include the main facts and feelings of the other person in your summary.

The BLS can be used in many situations in and around school—individual conferences with a student, parent-teacher conferences, discussions among staff and administrators, formulation of a problem in a class, interactions with colleagues. Regardless of the situation, you will find the pacing skills of the BLS invaluable.

References

Aspy, D., & Roebuck, F. (1977). *Kids don't learn from people they don't like.* Amherst, MA: Human Resource Development Center.

Faraday, S., & Harris, R. (1994). *Learning support, a staff development resource pack for those working with learners who have special needs.* London, England: Firther Education Unit, Training Agency, National Bureau of Students with Disabilities.

Gordon, T. (1974). *Teacher effectiveness training.* New York: David McKay.

Ivey, A. (1971). *Microcounseling: Innovations in interviewing.* Springfield, IL: Charles C Thomas.

Ivey, A. (1994). *Intentional interviewing and counseling: Facilitating development in a multicultural society.* Pacific Grove, CA: Brooks/Cole.

Ivey, A. Gluckstern, N., & Ivey, M. (1993). *Basic attending skills* (3rd ed.). North Amherst, MA: Microtraining.

5

Focusing

The concept of focusing has deep historical and psychological roots. Focusing has been used for thousands of years as a way of calming the mind and relaxing the body. Various meditative traditions and teachers often describe the undisciplined mind as a "drunken, restless monkey stung by a scorpion and possessed by a demon" (Ornish, 1990, p. 235). By quieting down and removing the disturbances in our minds, we are better able to concentrate on reality and deal with our real and perceived problems with greater clarity and effectiveness.

Practically applied to problems, successful focusing usually gives us a much better understanding of the true elements and causes of a problem. Many of our problems result from preconceptions and stereotypes about people and things. Focusing at its deepest level frequently enables you and the individuals with whom you are interacting to experience an actual shift that often helps release some of the "stuckness" that previously prevented you from solving the problem. By focusing on different aspects of the problem and reframing it, you become more capable of examining the problem in its totality, and a wider range of solutions is then possible (Ivey, Ivey, & Simek-Morgan, 1993).

An Illustration of Focusing as a Communication Skill

Focusing is best described through example. The teachers' union president, Jim Sinden, comes in to talk to you, the superintendent, about a breakdown in contract talks. Jim says, "The teachers are upset because, as you know, we're at an impasse with contract negotiations. Andy Reimann called the board president and they got into an argument that resulted in the president's hanging up. Now Andy calls me and asks what we should do next."

As you can sense, there are many possible ways in which you could respond to Jim's worried statement. You could attend to Jim or ignore him. You could use any of the skills of the basic listening sequence to draw out the problem in more detail. All of the above can be helpful. Each one leads Jim in a different direction. In addition to the communication skills already presented, you could also try focusing. Used in conjunction with open-ended questions, active listening, and the other communication skills, focusing can expand the range of problem solving to its maximum potential.

Two alternatives for response to Jim include the following:

Focus on the person: "Jim, you look really worried. What do you think we should do?" (reflection of feeling, open question).
Focus on the problem: "Contract problems again?" (encourage) or "Tell me what issues are stalling contract negotiations?" (open question).

Each different focus will lead Jim to talk about the problem from a different perspective. As a skilled superintendent, you want to keep Jim, the person, involved. At the same time, you need more data on the problem. If you are working with a serious recurring concern such as this, it can be well worthwhile to take time to study the difficulty through careful focus analysis.

Three additional areas of focus analysis are possible and useful in problem conception and definition.

Focus on others: The board president and other members of the board. For example, "What does the board president see as causing the problem?" Consider all people who might be related to the problem.
Focus on context: Context focus represents examining broader issues not readily apparent, such as the board's concerns about the current mood of the voters in the district. The history of relationships and possible conflict between the two groups is another example of contextual focus. For example, "Could you give me a rundown of what's been decided so far in the contract talks, what are the chief sticking

points, and who on the board is having the biggest problems with the teachers' demands?"

Focus on self: You as the superintendent are an expert in many
situations. As part of focus analysis, it is important to include yourself and your expertise as part of the analysis.
"My experience with this type of problem is _____.
Here's what I would suggest: _____."

If you as a superintendent want to understand a problem fully,
you need to lead the problem definition through use of the basic
listening sequence, the five stages of the problem-solving model
(chapter 7), and focus analysis. In this way, you can ensure that you
and your staff consider the full complexity of any issue.

Focus analysis is a simple concept that helps break down complex problems into useful, workable dimensions. You, as the administrator, can then coordinate the several areas of definition into
a working solution. At the same time, focus analysis is also very
complex. It is at the heart of postmodern theory, which stresses that
we need to recognize complexity, possibility, and multiple alternatives in our world.

Focusing in the Classroom

Focusing also can be used effectively in the presentation of any
well-planned lesson. Determining what you are trying to accom-
plish when you put together a class presentation can be richly en-
hanced by the addition of focusing. For example, when thinking
about a unit on the senses, one obviously must focus on the content
or the material to be covered. But other foci are frequently pertinent and can add to the substance and quality of the effort:

The multicultural perspective: What can be presented that will
be pertinent to the ethnic and gender diversity in the classroom?

Its integration with other subject areas: Asking how the senses
relate to the arts or the study of mathematics might yield
some fruitful connections. For example, one can construct
an art lesson based on the impact of color on sight.

Different modes of presentation: Lecturing is one way of presenting the material but cooperative learning, hands-on activities, field trips, role playing, and having visitors present
aspects of the material are some other alternatives.

Focusing can be a valuable resource in class discussions or one-
to-one interactions. As we saw in chapter 4, selectively focusing on
what you want to paraphrase often can help guide a discussion
toward particular emphases or relevant points. Also, as we examined in chapter 3, questioning skills are a highly selective way of
facilitating the movement toward a higher-order resolution of ten-
tative conclusions, insights, and dawning realizations. Focusing
through questioning encourages teachers to ponder what students
think and believe. Besides demonstrating an interest in what the
student has to say, thoughtful questions that examine different
viewpoints push the limits of students' assumptions and instill in
them a belief that they are an active, valued agent in their own
quest for answers.

Good thinking requires students to think independently, be intellectually curious, and try to empathize with others' viewpoints
that are different from their own. By introducing different foci, students will develop the dispassionateness and intellectual humility
that come from realizing that there are many different ways of
looking at an issue or problem.

The application of focusing in the classroom is a constant attempt to go after the essence of whatever it is that one is pursuing
at the time. That can be accomplished only by exploring and sort-
ing out the diversity of discourse implicit in any intellectual en-
deavor. Teachers who provide a variety of foci help students probe
beneath the surface of things and arrive at independent conclusions that come from their own reasoning.

Exercises in Focusing

1. Think through alternative foci. Here is a statement that you,
the principal, might receive from a teacher during a performance
review.

Charlotte: "It wasn't my fault that the report was in late. It was Marge's fault. She's always in the way. The report wasn't that important anyway. You never really told me when you wanted it."

Say to yourself or write down alternative foci. Note how what seems at first to be a simple person problem expands in complexity.

Person?
Problem?
Others?
Context?
Self?

2. Take focusing to your own work setting. The next time a friend or colleague approaches you about a problem he or she needs to solve, rather than give a quick response and answer immediately, take time to focus on the several dimensions of the problem. Which dimensions of focus come most easily to you? Which are most difficult?

Most often, moving beyond the immediate problem to be solved to contextual issues is most difficult. Yet it is this broad contextual thinking that most often produces the most satisfactory problem-solving session.

3. Use focusing in lesson preparation. Try to think through as many perspectives as possible in preparing a class lesson or unit. Address the purposes of the lesson by looking at various audiences, how it can be presented, and what you bring to it.

4. Class discussion and focusing. For the next class discussion try to introduce as many different foci as you can. For example, play devil's advocate on occasion, ask questions that will lead the students toward a different formulation of the issue or problem being considered, and bring in other perspectives where possible. Some of the higher-order questions listed in chapter 3 may be helpful.

References

Ivey, A., Ivey, M., & Simek-Morgan, L. (1993). *Counseling and psychotherapy: A multicultural perspective* (3rd ed.). Boston: Allyn & Bacon.

Ornish, D. (1990). *Dr. Dean Ornish's program for reversing heart disease.* New York: Random House.

6

Seven Influencing Skills

For both teachers and administrators, influencing skills play a major role in their effectiveness as helping agents, instructors, and managers. This chapter presents seven influencing skills that are effective in the leading process. Each influencing skill presented here leads most effectively if embedded within the structure of careful listening represented by attending behavior, observation of nonverbal behavior, and the basic listening sequence.

The seven influencing skills are listed in Table 6.1 in terms of the amount of control they require in the classroom, meeting, or two-person contact.

Influencing Skills in the Classroom

Influencing skills can be used effectively as long as they are balanced with the other communication skills we have presented. As a general rule, it is best to use leading skills that involve a minimum of control over the other person. But you will find that each person with whom you work responds differently—and to make it more complicated, the same person will respond differently at different times. Flexibility counts.

The following are some alternative ways of using the influencing skills, with commentary on their value and ordering.

Feedback

"John, when you pick on George it makes it difficult for me to teach my lesson. I have to constantly stop the class to talk to you and it bothers me that it's putting the class further and further behind."

TABLE 6.1 The Seven Influencing Skills

Influencing Skills	*Amount of Control Over Others*
Feedback Telling others how their actions are perceived by you and others	Modest
Information and explanation Providing specific facts, ideas, opinions, with the purpose of informing rather than "telling"	
Interpretation Reframing a problem or situation from a new point of view	Moderate
Self-disclosure Sharing your own ideas and past experience	
Advice Instructing a person what to do, what actions to take (the person may or may not follow advice)	
Direction Directing others to take a specific course of action	Extensive
Warnings or threats Pointing out clearly to others the consequences of actions	

Source: Ivey & Gluckstern, 1984; Ivey, Gluckstern, & Ivey, 1993.

Ideally, feedback should be specific and concrete. Without putting the person on the defensive, you want to communicate what it is that concerns you, its effect on you, and how the person's actions make you feel. By sticking to the facts rather than pointing a finger at the person, you are remaining nonjudgmental. It may be important to detail concrete examples of similar situations, but the important thing is for the student not to feel accused or that you are somehow blaming him for his actions. Simply communicating its impact on you is a reasonable and nonvolatile way to tell people how their actions affect you and others.

Information and Explanation

When providing information and explanations, it is again important to be concrete and specific. First, be clear and direct in what you say. Remember, you likely know more than the other person. Can they understand you? Enrich your information with concrete and highly specific examples. Finally, ask the other person to paraphrase back to you what you have just said. This step is particularly important for complicated information.

Frequently, this influencing skill will come into play when a teacher presents materials to either the whole class or individual students. Often, the teacher's role as a provider of useful and helpful information plays into this skill, because children need the facilitation and encouragement from a skilled, knowledgeable adult, one who can influence them in positive ways.

Interpretation

Hearing is a combination of sound plus interpretation. We hear sounds with our ears, but we always interpret those sounds personally, depending on who we are and our deeply held beliefs and contexts. Reframing is the offering of a new context, a way of thinking about something differently so that new insights and ideas can take hold. Interpreting what we see, hear, and experience from a new frame of reference helps all parties reexamine and think through the situation from another perspective. Thus interpretation is oriented toward giving new ways to look at old information.

When teachers are working with students, they can present alternative outlooks for the same event or happening. For example, English teachers can invite students to look at different ways a character's actions in a novel might be interpreted. At that time, they could also discuss how different characters might have different points of view depending upon their gender, social class, political persuasion, or religion.

The richest interpretations are based on the widest possible consideration of evidence. Teachers can help students in their thinking by helping them recognize their interpretations and consider new interpretations in light of new evidence.

The roots of interpretation lie in creativity, the ability to make something new from what already exists. Creativity demands that one be able to view things from a new and different perspective, assemble existing pieces into new wholes, and take things apart and reconstruct a new picture—perhaps more complete and descriptive than what existed before. The essence of divergent thinking lies in one's ability to reconfigure reality in ways not previously constructed. Often a dispute between two students can be resolved by looking at what the conflict was really about and how the two can restructure their relationship, using new insights or different assumptions about the other and what is possible between them.

Similarly, teachers who ask the kinds of questions that begin with "What if" or "Have you thought of" stimulate the kind of divergent thinking that produces future problem solvers and idea generators. Playing with ideas or concepts is the essence of creative, constructive thinking. For example, the playfulness of scientists, like the playfulness of children, is intense, allowing both to explore and try out a wide range of ideas with no fear of being wrong.

Self-Disclosure

Using self-disclosure can help a student see that the teacher has experienced or shares some of the same kinds of problems that the student is experiencing. For example, the following dialogue demonstrates the use of self-disclosure and active listening when a teacher is trying to help a student prepare for an oral report:

Student: Do I have to get up in front of everybody?

Teacher: It's making you a little nervous to make your report to the class?

Student: Well, what happens if I can't remember what to say?

Teacher: That happened to me once. I got up there and my mind went blank. I just went back to my notes to see what I said last and that seemed to help.

Student: So I can take my notes up with me?

Teacher: Definitely. No problem.

Self-disclosure, used in moderation and in the right context, helps make you seem more like a real person and can be very supportive in the process of mentoring. It can be a good way of helping a student see that almost everyone shares the same problems, anxieties, concerns, and triumphs. Overused, however, such "I statements" can tend to get boring and be a distraction to the task at hand.

Advice

It is very tempting for a teacher to give advice to students. However, unless it is directly solicited and seems appropriate to the occasion, well-meaning advice may be ignored or come across as "If I were you, _____."

If you have a good rapport with students, they might be inclined to discuss with you some personal matters that are troubling them. For example, the following conversation took place in a sixth-grade classroom between the teacher and one of his students. Notice how he subtly reinforces or "gives" advice by listening reflectively, asking questions, and gently leading the student to a solution that fits the situation:

Student: What if you like a guy and he's on drugs and you don't know about it until he takes them out and says, "Here, have some."

Teacher: When you're running with a crowd and they call you chicken for not taking them, it takes an awful lot of courage, doesn't it?

Student: I'd say, "No, forget it."

Teacher: Do you think drugs are all right?

Student: No.

Teacher: O.K., so if you really thought a lot of this person what would be a good thing to do for that person?

Student: We can't tattle on him.

Teacher: O.K. Maybe you don't want to tattle. What could you do?

Student: We couldn't try and help him get off it—

Teacher: Why?

Student: We couldn't do it.

Teacher: Why?

Student: Because they have a mind of their own.

Teacher: I think if you really like a person you'd try and help him, wouldn't you?

(CBS News, 1972, *What's New at School*)

Direction

Actual directives to a student can be useful, but if used in excess, especially in the teaching of writing, they can be a reversion to the old "search and destroy" approach to evaluating a student's paper by pointing out all the mistakes. Used judiciously, directives can be helpful to a student. She can benefit from a well-placed piece of information, especially if the directive is objective and nonevaluative.

Warnings or Threats

The strongest influencing skill, it should be used sparingly. Inherent in a warning or threat are the logical consequences of failure to act ("Stephen, if you do this, then the consequence will be _____"). For example, if a student is consistently not turning in his homework you might say, "If you don't get your homework in, I'll have to give you a zero." The use of threats or warnings also requires calmness and good attending skills so that students don't end up feeling fearful, submissive, or hostile.

Integration of Attending and Influencing Skills

The following is part of the transcript of a writing conference with a fifth-grade student. Notice the number of times the teacher effectively switches back and forth from attending to influencing skills.

Teacher: "So, Carlos, you are writing a story about your mother and the things she likes?" (Summarization)

Student: "Yeah. Just the outline of my mother and then on the inside write what she likes and doesn't like."

Teacher: "That's nice. I like that." (Affirmation)

Student: "She likes to swim. She likes to play sports like baseball."

Teacher: "Um. So your mother likes to play a lot of sports like swimming and baseball." (Acknowledgment and paraphrase)

Student: "She swims almost every day if she can."

Teacher: "What kind, what are you going to use to symbolize the swimming?" (Open-ended question)

Student: "Just like waves and water—"

Teacher: "O.K. Waves would be nice. Could you tell me whether there is anything she doesn't like?" (Affirmation, open-ended question)

Student: "Yeah, snakes."

Teacher: "O.K., same as me, huh!" (Self-disclosure)

Student: "I don't like snakes either."

Teacher: "Did you know that lots of people seem to be bothered by snakes?" (Information and explanation)

Student: "My next door neighbor has two pet snakes."

Teacher: "So let's get back to your writing. Your writing is really a letter to your mother?" (Refocus)

Student: "Yes."

Teacher: "Let's see how you go about your letter. See if we have to make any revisions. Would you want to read it for me?" (Direction and open-ended question)

Student: "'Dear Mom, Thank you very much for sacrificing your sports to have me into this world. As I grow up I hope to jog, swim, play baseball, and do all the things you did when I wasn't born. Thank you for bringing me into this world.'"

Teacher: "Ah! That's nice, Carlos. That's neat. What do you really like about what you wrote? There's a couple things I really like. I just want to know what you really like. What sentence, what words stand out in your mind?" (Affirmation, feedback, open-ended questions)

Basic to all leading, whether the more modest feedback or the strongly worded warning, is that of giving clear and effective directions.

Giving directions is one of the most basic teaching skills. In giving directions (and in all influencing and leading skills to some degree) it is important that you:

1. Know what you want to have happen. Clear goals are very important.
2. Express what you want to say concretely and clearly.
3. Check to see if what you said was understood. Make arrangements as necessary to follow up and see if something happened as a result of your direction.

These same three points can be applied to all influencing skills. In particular, use these ideas when giving feedback, interpreting, or providing warnings or threats.

And, of all these dimensions in leading, perhaps the most important is your willingness and ability to follow up with your students, colleagues, and staff.

Exercises in Leading and Influencing

1. When working with students in conferencing situations or small groups, try using a balance of attending and influencing skills. Remember that your ability to lead is based on good attending behavior and the pacing skills of the basic listening sequence.

2. Practice direction giving. Most basic to leading are the three points on directions. Consider your own classroom or school. What directions do you have to give in your position? (a) Do you know what you want to have happen? (b) Are you clear, concrete, and specific in direction giving? (c) Do you follow up and check whether the other party or student understands what you want? Test out these concepts the next time you give directions.

3. Skill practice. Each of the influencing skills presented in this chapter requires study and practice to arrive at mastery. Select one

skill at a time and test out its effectiveness in different situations. Remember the importance of flexibility and being able to change the skill—don't get caught with only one or two leadership skills.

References

CBS News. (1972). *What's new at school.*

Ivey, A., & Gluckstern, N. (1984). *Basic influencing skills.* North Amherst, MA: Microtraining.

Ivey, A., Gluckstern, N., & Ivey, M. (1993). *Basic attending skills* (3rd ed.). North Amherst, MA: Microtraining.

7

Organizing Communication and Problem-Solving Skills for "Win-Win" Solutions

Conflict is an inevitable part of life. Everyone who works and lives together inevitably gets into disagreements or differences of opinion about how to deal with the many issues and concerns we face constantly. A fundamental problem in schools today is the relative ineffectiveness of how conflict is dealt with. Many students' and teachers' needs are not being met and much frustration and unhappiness follows.

All too often conflicts in the school are resolved in terms of "I win—you lose." The teacher or principal may exact compliance by forceful disciplinary measures, but all too often the student will end up feeling resentful and at times hostile. Similar results can occur if the style of a principal is "top-down" or autocratic toward the staff.

The following is an example of a principal-teacher interaction that occurred recently in an elementary school:

Principal: "John, I'd like to see you in my office."

Teacher: "O.K. I'll be right there."

Principal: (closes door when teacher arrives) "John, did you get my permission first before inviting that reporter to the school?"

Teacher: "Well, our team talked about it and we all agreed that that was the best time for him to come."

Principal: "From now on I want you to clear visitors with me first. Do you know what kind of possible disruption this might cause? On that day we're going to have eight substitutes in here! The place could be chaotic."

Teacher: "The reporter was just going to come to my room, observe a few students, and leave."

Principal: "I don't care. I want you to tell me first before you invite anyone into the school. Is that understood?"

Instead of using a confrontational, "I win—you lose" approach, how might the principal have presented it? We shall take the communication skills of pacing and leading and integrate them into a five-stage problem-solving model as a way to help avoid conflict and develop "win-win" solutions.

The Five-Stage Problem-Solving Model

Here we present a way to organize communication skills in a systematic fashion that will allow you and other people to work together. There are five key aspects of a problem-solving model that can be integrated with pacing and leading skills. We will move between individual and group meetings. As the five-stage structure is reviewed, it also should be noted that the structure here will be useful in a difficult or complex parent conference (Ivey, Ivey, & Simek-Morgan, 1993; Ivey & Matthews, 1984).

Stage 1: Rapport and Structuring

When you start a meeting or, in this case, a dialogue, your first task is to provide an environment in which all parties feel comfortable and safe. Through the use of attending behavior, especially through the recognition of eye contact, let the person know that you are aware of his or her presence. Attending is basic to rapport. What the principal in the above example could have done was to take time for informal conversation, assume a relaxed stance, and try to acknowledge the teacher's presence. Offering something, like a cup of coffee or tea, is often a gesture of inclusion that makes the person feel comfortable.

It is natural to want to jump right into the problem to be solved, especially if either person is upset or agitated. However, to provide balance and structure, initially lay out your agenda and the purpose of the meeting. Clearly this is a leading skill; providing a statement of structure at the beginning of the session is perhaps your most important leadership function in meetings. And, as you provide this structure, encourage the other person to participate in agenda setting.

With John, for example, once rapport is established, it may be helpful to outline the issue by briefly saying you'd like to understand things a bit better. And—because the issue is important to both of you—you want to start with a clear understanding of issues and goals before moving to problem solving.

With the structure suggested here, you might wish to tell John that first you will define the problem and then the goals for the meeting, and then alternative solutions will be generated. Finally, you can tell the person or people with whom you are meeting that one or more alternatives for concrete action will be selected.

In this way, you have not told your audience how to behave or what to decide. Rather, you have provided them with an open structure for joint decision making.

Stage 2: Defining the Problem

Some meetings move immediately to solving problems without a clear awareness of the problem to be solved. Presenting the problem as something to be arrived at mutually is the first step to using good communication skills. For example, the principal could start off by saying: "John, I need to discuss with you the issue of visitors coming to the school. It seems that one was invited recently without my knowledge. I'd like to discuss my concerns about that, but I'd also like to hear from you about the details of the invitation and whether you feel that my concerns are justified." By immediately treating it as a mutual concern that will be discussed by both of them, the principal makes it far more likely that cooperation and openness will result in resolution of the problem.

As you begin to hear what the issues or conflicts are, you will find the basic listening sequence (BLS) very useful throughout the meeting. For example, you may want to paraphrase back what you are hearing and also use encourages. Acknowledgment of feelings can be helpful as well. Brief statements such as "Apparently you were really excited about having the reporter do the story about your class" can show that you are sensitively listening to what is being said by reflecting your awareness of emotions.

When the person has finished, you can summarize what he said. Periodically, stop and summarize what a person or group has been saying on a particular point, perhaps listing key ideas on newsprint. The summary does not indicate approval or acceptance of an idea, but rather a point of punctuation in which you as leader indicate that the idea or set of points has been noted and the meeting can now move on to another topic. The better you are at hearing the other person's point of view, the more possibility that your ideas will also be heard.

At the conclusion of Stage 2, a "super-summary" of the problem definition is usually helpful. Here you may wish to make a summary of summaries in which the key aspects of the problem definition are repeated and the other person or people can add their further clarification and explanation if necessary. It is important to note that this five-stage structure also can be useful with groups dealing with complex issues. In our example, you can say, "It appears, John, that you really find visitors a welcome addition to our program, but at the same time I want to make sure that we ensure the privacy and security of the school. Does that sound about right?"

Stage 3: Defining Goals

Too many meetings stop with problem definition. What you want to do is establish the context or reason for dealing with the problem in the first place. There is a saying that "If you don't know where you are going, you may end up somewhere else." Problem definition is not enough. What are the goals toward which your meeting is striving—both short term and long term?

You can introduce this stage of the meeting with a summary of the problem definition, followed by "Given this definition of the problem, what are our ideal goals for problem resolution?" or

"What do you want to have happen?" Or in this particular case, the principal could say to John, "I want to make sure we have a policy about visitors that accommodates all our needs and concerns."

Sometimes in the hurly-burly of a group meeting, some members may feel that their ideas have not been heard. They may be sitting back, no longer participating in the session. It is these people who can undermine the best of a problem-solving session.

At this point, it is useful to check in with each staff member and their current standing in the meeting. First, through the use of the summary, you can organize the facts and ideas of the session. You may want to summarize individual and group feelings about those facts, particularly if the meeting is hot and has produced controversy.

Then, follow the summary with direct eye contact aimed at each member of the group. Ask them their reactions to the problem definition and summary and if they have any criticisms, corrections of your summary, or other ideas to provide. Spend time bringing the group together to a consensus of problem definition and ideal goals.

Unless the members of the group are working together and each individual feels he or she has had some say, the long-term value of the meeting can be destroyed. Here again, you will find the BLS invaluable in bringing people and ideas together.

At times, a careful examination of goals will reveal that you and the other person or members of the group have different goals. Having clarity on differences is important before moving on to brainstorming or actual problem solving.

State 4: Generating Alternative Solutions

Many meetings actually start here. The leader of the meeting moves quickly with a problem definition, assumes that the ideal goal is implicit in his or her statement at the beginning of the session, and then moves to draw out answers and possibilities.

If you take time for rapport and structure your meeting carefully for clear problem and goal definition, you will find that group members are more willing to share their ideas in a participatory fashion. This is especially so if you have attempted to provide each individual with attention and support for their ideas and perceptions.

Again, you can use the summary and BLS to structure this portion of the meeting. You may say, for example, "So far we've defined our problem as _____ and our goal in working it through is _____—now what occurs to you as possibilities to bring the two together?

What has happened here is that you have provided a clear structure for generation of alternatives. The open question invites everyone to participate. Once again you can use the skills of encouraging, paraphrasing, and acknowledging feelings to draw out each member's ideas about the future.

The fourth stage of the meeting is where you will most likely be sharing your ideas. But first let the group see what can be generated. Bring in your own ideas gently so as not to disturb a working group. In going back to the original example, if John has agreed on what the problem is and what the goals are, he will be more amenable to helping establish a sound policy for visitors that will accommodate not only the principal's needs and concerns but also his own interests. Some of the solutions to the problem could be that all visitors report to the office first, that teachers let the office know when they will be having visitors, or that the principal actively supports and helps plan for the inclusion of worthwhile visitors.

You may find it helpful to summarize and list each alternative generated. If you do not summarize new ideas and indicate that they have been acknowledged, you will often find the group member repeating the same idea again and again until it is noted. Or a member whose idea is not noted might slump back in a chair and fail to participate further. Clearly, this fourth stage is similar to creative brainstorming, which people use to solve all sorts of problems, whether individual or institutional.

Once the group or you and the other person have generated a suitable number of alternatives, it is time for commitment to action. Too many meetings and planning sessions break up before this important step.

Stage 5: Commitment to Action

If the hard work of the session or meeting is not to be wasted and the ideas you came up with are to be followed, specific action steps are needed. It is here that your leadership is most necessary. Although pacing skills are perhaps most critical in the first four phases, your ability to lead must be manifested at this time.

Leading a meeting is not necessarily telling your staff what to do, however. Clearly, telling people what to do seldom works! If the action alternatives have been clearly summarized, the focused question, "Which alternative or alternatives should we act on?" can bring about joint decision making.

As you can anticipate, the BLS will be useful in prioritizing your plan of action. Each individual in the meeting will have feelings about what the implementation plan should look like, and you will want to paraphrase and reflect their thoughts and feelings. Through careful pacing, you can often move the group to a consensus that all can accept and later support. This consensus is especially important in developing an educational plan for students or implementing an important new policy.

Once you decide on what will be done, specific individuals can volunteer or be assigned to various tasks. If the meeting has used the talents of the entire group and has allowed full participation, assigning staff to various parts of the task may not be necessary. Their participation in the meeting often will indicate to you and to them who should take over which part of the task.

The meeting can close with a summary of what has happened: the problem definition, the goals, the key alternatives generated and decided upon, and the specific individuals who are to complete each task.

This final summary is tempting to omit because most likely you and the group members will be tired and will want to adjourn the meeting. But taking time carefully to summarize what has happened will facilitate later action. Also, you will want to see if what you have set up is working successfully. For example, are all visitors now reporting to the office and are you doing your part in facilitating the agenda of any of the teachers' guests?

At some future date you might also want to see how the individuals feel about the agreed-upon plan. For example, in a few weeks you can touch base with John and find out whether he is happy with the way visitors are now being handled.

Conflicts Within the Classroom

Conflicts within a classroom have many of the same characteristics as the principal-teacher conflict illustrated above. Teachers
often feel as if they have only two alternatives in maintaining control—either being strict or adopting a permissive, democratic atmosphere. Thus teachers often unconsciously face two choices in
dealing with their students: either they're "hard-nosed" and run a
"tight ship" or they "give in" and try to accommodate the students.

The following scenario illustrates an all-too-frequent situation in
a classroom: You have just broken your class of fifth graders into
small groups and have begun teaching your prize unit on the Aztecs,
but, to your exasperation, the class seems restless and out of sorts.
You try walking around the room, waiting for quiet, and finally
you turn to a group of boys who are talking and say rather sharply,
"Stop talking this minute and move your desks away from each
other!" The boys look at you with a rather startled expression and
then rather slowly follow your orders, giggling as they do so. One
of the boys "accidentally" drops a book as he pushes his seat across
the room and another bumps into his friend's desk as he moves,
scratching the top rather badly. You notice that the other students
appear rather listless and unhappy and do not seem to be looking
forward to your presentation on the Aztecs.

Obviously, no one has really ended up feeling good about the
interaction. The other solution would have been for the teacher to
"give in" by simply going on with the lesson with the talking going
on, but that also wouldn't really have resolved the problem, because then the teacher's needs would not have been met.

Rarely are teachers completely authoritarian or permissive in
their approach to discipline. However, most tend to lean toward
the former, if only because the norm in most schools is control and
"keeping students quiet." It is also possible to maintain control in
an "open" or integrated classroom. This middle approach, which
balances openness and control, is what we would like to focus on.

When teachers use the five-stage problem-solving model in a
classroom, they are dealing with students in a way that does not
involve the use of either covert or actual power. Furthermore,

teachers and students listen to one another and the seeds for real communication begin to emerge. It is also worth noting that many times when teachers discipline students, they do it on the basis of a quick and cursory assessment of the situation and may not fully grasp what the issues are. For example, during class a teacher may yell at a student for "receiving" a note she thinks was sent by another student, when the contents turn out to be a congratulatory message from another student's parent on winning a science contest.

When teachers invite students to be part of the solution to a problem, the students feel more respected and included and thus are more highly motivated to act responsibly. Simply ordering students to behave in certain ways does not allow them to internalize such commands because they are subsequently too busy feeling defensive, resentful, or resistant to the orders. When teachers treat students with respect and take the time to listen attentively to them, especially when the teacher first states decisively what's bothering him or her, students tend to respond positively because they are being treated as responsible, capable, mature, and worthy of esteem.

Let's come back to the original conflict of the Aztec presentation in the fifth-grade class and document the following dialogue that takes place between the class and the teacher who is now using the five-stage problem-solving model and the basic listening sequence:

Teacher: "Class, it seems that things aren't going too well right now and I want to take a few minutes to talk the matter over with you."

Student: "He's being a brat again!"

Teacher: "When all of you are talking and not listening it makes me feel frustrated and as if no one cares about what I'm saying. Then I fall behind and worry that we won't finish in time for our class trip."

Student: "When are we going to go outside?"

Teacher: "I'd like to hear from you for a minute about what we can do about the noise and people not listening. Could anyone come up with any suggestions at this point for what we can do?"

Student: "Give us a break."

Teacher: "O.K. That's one idea. I'm going to write them on the board. Who has some other suggestions?"

Student: "Let us get into small groups more."

Teacher: "So you'd like to work more together in teams. Is that it?"

Student: "Yeah, but put the talkers in separate groups."

Teacher: "That's really two ideas—working more in small groups and placing the talkers in separate groups."

Student: "They bother us and then we can't get our work done."

Teacher: "It seems that you feel that some people do all the talking."

Student: "Yeah, like Julie."

Student: "I do not!"

Teacher: "We have three ideas up here now. What else can anyone think of?"

Student: "Write down the names of the people who talk on the board and then keep them in during playground time."

Teacher: "You're suggesting that they should be punished for talking."

Student: "That's it."

Teacher: "Some other ideas?"

Student: "Give them a zero on their next test."

Teacher: "O.K. Give them a zero. I have that one down."

Student: "How about if we have a rule of no talking when the teacher is talking?"

Teacher: "Sounds good to me! Anyone else?"

Student: "Maybe do more stuff like making things or drawing charts or pictures. Sometimes I get kind of bored."

Teacher: "If I'm hearing you correctly, you feel bored sometimes about the lesson and you'd like to get into more activities."

Student: "Well, kind of."

Student: "What if we could just talk quietly and listen at the same time?"

Teacher: "You'd like to be able to talk while I'm talking, is that right?"

Student: "Ah, well I guess not really. Maybe we could raise our hands first."

Teacher: "What other ideas does anyone have?" (There are no others.) "O.K., so let's see what we have at this point. Let's cross out any of the ones that we don't like. I don't really care for #4, where people whose names are on the board have to stay in during recess."

Student: "I don't think giving a zero to talkers is a good idea."

Teacher: "I'll take that off also. Also, someone already rejected #8, which is allowing everyone to talk while I'm talking. That leaves 1, 2, 3, 6, 7, and 9. Does anyone want to add anything at this point?"

Student: "When can we do some of the small-group activities?"

Teacher: "As soon as I finish what we're doing today. I'll type up this list, we can go over it tomorrow, and at that time we can talk about how we're going to put these ideas into action."

There is no longer the confrontational "me against them" power struggle in this example. The conflict and the problems it has caused the teacher are being solved rationally, democratically, and with the full participation of everyone. No one is exercising power over anyone else, and the students are being included in a give-and-take atmosphere. Everyone, not just the teacher, worked at solving the problem, and because the students were included they were more likely to have the motivation to implement the ideas. Also, at least one hidden but significant problem came out—at least one of the students was bored by the teacher's presentation and suggested some hands-on participation, which the teacher will try to implement.

Needless to say, it takes a personally strong, confident teacher to engage students in this fashion. However, listening and openness are signs of individual strength and power—and a way to gain real influence with your students.

The five-stage problem-solving model can be universally applied in countless situations both in and outside the classroom. Indeed, any relationship involving people—such as friendships, community interactions, marriages, and business relationships— can benefit from careful problem solving. The growing field of mediation is one example of an area where these ideas can be effectively applied. By defining what the problem or issue is and then actively listening to the parties involved, people have resolved many conflicts that otherwise would have ended up on a negative or unsatisfactory note.

Teachers can use this model either in a whole-class situation, as illustrated above, or in one-to-one interactions with students. And the five-stage model can be used in many different contexts, from setting up classroom rules and regulations to issues relating to students' needs involving the curriculum. For example, it could be used in the case of a student who will miss a test because of an off-site sports event. It also could be used productively with students who have special learning needs.

When teachers tell their class what's bothering them and then actively listen to what the students' needs are by using the five-stage problem-solving model and the BLS, they can create solutions to problems that are acceptable to everyone and where no one ends up being the loser.

Exercises in Problem Solving

1. Use the five stages in a one-to-one contact. The next time a colleague comes to you for assistance with a problem, systematically think through and apply the five stages suggested here. Develop rapport, draw out the problem and the ideal goal, generate alternatives, and obtain a commitment to action.

In this process, attempt to use only the BLS so that your colleague is able to generate the solution on her or his own. Only provide specific suggestions and advice when absolutely necessary. Attempt to confine advice and suggestions to the fourth stage of the model.

2. Observe a meeting. Most meetings are much more disorganized than is necessary. Use the following checklist to analyze some conditions of the effective meeting. What worked in the session you observed? What was missing?

It is not necessary to follow each step of the five-stage structure in every meeting in an exact progression or order, but you will find that the most effective meetings at some point include all of the following dimensions.

Key ingredients of effective meetings:

    a. *Rapport and structuring.* Was there recognition of each person present through eye contact and good attending skills? Did the leader provide some sort of systematic structure for the session?

    b. *Defining the problem.* Was the problem clearly defined? Did the leader allow each group member to express his or her ideas of what the problem was? Did the leader acknowledge feelings around key ideas and issues? Was the leader able to summarize the problem or opportunity clearly as defined by the group?

    c. *Defining goals.* Was the ideal problem resolution discussed, even if not fully attainable? Was some effort made to involve each member in problem definition and goal setting?

    d. *Generating alternative solutions.* Did the leader encourage and accept varying ideas? Was each member encouraged to provide input? Were at least three alternatives considered? (You don't have a choice unless you have at least three options.)

    e. *Commitment to action.* Did the meeting break up without clear plans for follow up? Did the leader ensure that the next steps were clear and that individuals were selected to act on jointly agreed-on goals? Was there a final meeting summary statement?

3. Conduct a meeting yourself. Use the outline above. It is especially critical that you use the basic listening sequence and involve each single member present at the meeting throughout each stage of the process. Be especially sure to include Stage 5 and plan for follow-up, or new ideas and plans may vanish.

4. When a disagreement or a conflict arises in your class, try using the five-stage model for resolving the issue. Explain that it is a new way of solving a problem and that you and the class will work together to solve it.

5. The next time you have a problem or issue involving one of your students that needs to be presented in a parent-teacher

conference, try to use the five-stage problem-solving approach and the basic listening skills sequence when you are dealing with the parent. Try to listen attentively, encourage, and reflect feelings as you work with them on the five-stage outline.

References

Ivey, A., Ivey, M., & Simek-Morgan, L. (1993). *Counseling and psychotherapy: A multicultural perspective* (3rd ed.). Boston: Allyn & Bacon.

Ivey, A., & Matthews, W. (1984). A meta-model for structuring the clinical interview. *Journal of Counseling and Development, 63,* 237-243.

8

Alternatives to Violence: Developing a Mediation Program

The society we live in is one of the most violent in the world. The high level of violence among our people is in part a response to the violence embedded in our institutions and our values. The statistics are mind numbing. Overall, the United States has the highest rate of interpersonal violence and the highest homicide rate of all the countries in the industrial world. Handgun deaths in 1985 stood at over 8,000 in this country, whereas Japan had 46, Switzerland 31, Israel 18, Great Britain 8, and Australia 5. And weapons possession alone does not necessarily increase a country's homicide rate. In Switzerland, because all adult males are required to serve in the military reserve until age 50, all are required by law to bear arms. Consequently, almost all Swiss homes contain guns and most Swiss citizens have access to guns. Yet few Swiss citizens use guns to kill one another. In addition, it is estimated that each year we spend $60 billion on violence-related injuries (Prothrow-Stith, 1991, p. 15).

A recent survey by the New York State United Teachers reported an overwhelming increase in discipline problems over the last 5 years. More than 10,000 teachers had been the victims of on-the-job violence, with nearly one fourth of those hurt seriously enough to miss time from work. Ninety-one percent of union leaders report that they've heard more swearing from students over the last 5 years, and 87% see more defiant attitudes among the children they teach. A total of 5% of students—and 21% of those with poor grades—said they had threatened a teacher in some way.

Every study and survey shows that students are constantly exposed to and assaulted by violence. One quarter to one third of high school students have been beaten at school and almost all have witnessed a beating. Even more alarming is the fact that more than half of the high school students in one study had witnessed a shooting (C. Johnson, 1995, p. 30).

A recent survey by Metropolitan Life showed that two in five students believe that their school does an only fair or poor job of providing safe and secure school grounds, with high school students the most likely to assess their school negatively (52%).

One of the reasons for feeling insecure is the prevalence of handguns in this country. According to the National Rifle Association, approximately 200 million firearms are in the hands of American private citizens. Others put the estimate as high as 400 million. One to three million of these are large-clip, high-rate-of-fire automatic and semiautomatic assault weapons. According to the Justice Department's Bureau of Justice Statistics, 70% of the more than 24,000 homicides committed in 1993 involved firearms, and four out of five were committed with handguns. More than 1 million Americans faced an assailant armed with a gun during 1993. And youth are now settling their disputes more and more with shootings rather than with fists, often with deadly results.

It is estimated that between 135,000 and 270,000 guns are carried to school every day by students (American Psychological Association, 1993, p. 26). The National Education Association calculates that on any given day, about 160,000 students stay home because of fear of violence in or on the way to school, and a 1994 Gallup poll found that two thirds of all teenagers said their "best friends" had been physically harmed in the last 12 months.

Students' Reactions to Violence in the Schools

The voices of the students themselves reflect how violence is affecting their lives. The following are children's responses to an invitation by the *Cleveland Plain Dealer* in Cleveland, Ohio to write about the violence they experience in their lives (Levey, 1994, pp. C-4-C-5):

Sharon has this to say about the threat of violence in her life:

"Is there any hope left? Too many people are dying before their time. Every day I wake up and I wonder if I will make it another day. Will somebody try to take something that is mine? Part of the problem is too much jealousy. Kids get jealous and want to take what is yours. That causes conflict. I have seen too many of my friends die because of jealousy. When one of my close friends died, I felt like shooting the person who killed him. But that would be wrong. Then it would be two people gone. I just hope I won't be the next one."

Jason writes:

"Last month, my friend Johnny and my other friends got into a fight with another boy in school. They broke the boy's nose.

During the summer, my friend Freddie and my other friend were jumped by some boys at Martin Luther King Plaza. They put a gun to Freddie's head and took his jacket.

I think the violence in our community needs to be stopped and more policemen put on the streets to stop the violence."

Tasha says this about her experiences with violence:

"I have been afraid of just walking down the hall to get to another class because you don't know who is harmful. Someone can hurt you even if they look innocent. I don't get scared coming to and from school because I get a ride almost every day.

My solution to stop all violence: Don't have any weapons and treat everyone equally, no matter what color they are."

Our approach to conflicts in our society and in the legal profession in particular historically has been adversarial. Plaintiff and defendant, principal and student, employer and employee, or debaters of a highly charged social issue like abortion or gun control compete in a situation in which at least one party eventually loses. Seldom does such an approach effectively resolve the issue at hand. Even when one party is the "winner," both parties often end up losing. The one who lost often either avoids any future contact with the winner or tries to get even. This situation leads to even more conflict and animosity. Eventually the relationship either gets irreparably harmed or dies.

Alternatives-to-Violence Programs:
Mediation as a Key Option

Fortunately, there are programs and approaches that are beginning to deal with the epidemic of violence in the schools. In all
cases, teaching the basic elements of communication is essential for
their success.

Many schools are now beginning to confront the issue of violence by introducing antiviolence curricula, conflict resolution,
and conflict management. In a survey of 700 school districts conducted in 1994 by the National School Boards Association, it was
discovered that about 60% of the districts in their survey taught
students the skills of conflict resolution and peer mediation.
Nationwide, more than 2,000 schools conduct conflict-resolution
programs. And in some states, such as Illinois, conflict-resolution
training is now mandated (Sautter, 1995, p. K8).

Some schools are initiating conflict resolution training workshops such as the Alternatives to Violence Program (AVP), which
focus on students' attitudes toward conflict. AVP attempts to deal
constructively with the violence students find in their lives and its
influence on them. By learning communication skills like active
listening and the application of concepts like "I" messages and attending skills, students gradually learn to both view and handle
violence in different ways. Among other skills and concepts generally taught in such workshops are those of community building,
cooperation, affirmation, and problem solving, all essential to the
nonviolent resolution of conflicts.

Peer mediation is one of the more promising avenues in schools
for resolving conflicts peacefully and offering suitable alternatives
to violence. Mediation is a process by which one tries to get two
parties to arrive at a consensus through cooperative exploration. It
is being used more and more, not only in our court systems but
also in the schools. Students are resolving their differences through
discussion rather than argument, and through communication
rather than conflict. In mediation, there are no winners and losers,
but rather a mutually agreed-upon resolution of the issues between the participating parties.

In peer mediation, students rather than teachers can resolve conflicts and, more important, can orchestrate solutions that they, rather than external authorities, dictate. As many teachers and school administrators have found, "allowing students to be joint architects in matters affecting them promotes feelings of control and autonomy" (D. W. Johnson, Johnson, Dudley, & Burnett, 1992, p. 11). Consequently, students feel that they have more of an active, powerful role as part of the school community and are more motivated to become responsible, committed members of their peer group and school.

According to the National Association for Mediation in Education (N.A.M.E.), the central goals of school-based mediation are "to teach students how to deal with anger constructively, how to communicate feelings and concerns without using violence and abusive language, how to think critically about alternative solutions, and how to agree to solutions in which all parties win" (Kort, 1990, p. 15). Figure 8.1 lists 10 important reasons for using peer mediation.

How to Conduct Mediation Training

Setting up an all-school mediation program involves a combination of faculty awareness and support. It requires overall planning where one or more teachers agree to be the school coordinators. Training of 15 to 20 hours is needed for students chosen to be peer mediators and the faculty who will work with them. Although students and teachers can be trained separately, it is often advantageous to have them trained together. A group spirit of cooperation often develops and students, teachers, and administrators get to know each other as a working team.

Mediation training sessions generally combine a presentation of the foundation skills of mediation, which include exploring what conflict and violence mean to the group, practicing active or reflective listening, and discussing, demonstrating, and practicing various other communication skills, such as attending behavior and how to ask good questions.

1. Conflict is a natural human state, often accompanying changes in our institutions or personal growth. It is better approached with skills than avoidance.

2. More appropriate and effective systems are needed to deal with conflict in the school setting than expulsion, suspension, court intervention, and detention.

3. The use of mediation to resolve school-based disputes can result in improved communication between and among students, teachers, administrators, and parents and can, in general, improve the school climate as well as providing a forum for addressing common concerns.

4. The use of mediation as a conflict-resolution method can result in a reduction of violence, vandalism, chronic school absence, and suspension.

5. Mediation training helps both young people and teachers to deepen their understanding about themselves and others, and provides them with lifetime dispute-resolution skills.

6. Mediation training increases students' interest in conflict resolution, justice, and the American legal system, while encouraging a higher level of citizenship activity.

7. Shifting the responsibility for solving appropriate school conflicts from adults to young adults and children frees both teachers and administrators to concentrate more on teaching than on discipline.

8. Recognizing that young people are competent to participate in the resolution of their own disputes encourages student growth and gives students skills—such as listening, critical thinking, and problem solving—that are basic to all learning.

9. Mediation training, with its emphasis on listening to others' points of view and the peaceful resolution of differences, assists in preparing students to live in a multicultural world.

10. Mediation provides a system of problem solving that is uniquely suited to the personal nature of young people's problems and is frequently used by students for problems they would not take to parents, teachers, or principals. (Davis & Porter, 1985)

Figure 8.1 Why We Need Peer Mediation

Most training sessions spend considerable time going through the actual steps of a peer mediation session. Although there is considerable variation, Figure 8.2 outlines a basic training sequence.

1. Have the peer mediators introduce themselves as mediators to the disputants.
2. State the rules of the mediation hearing:
   - Agreement to solve the problem
   - No name-calling, swearing, or put-downs
   - No interrupting
   - Be as honest as you can
   - Speak directly to the mediators
3. Explain what mediation is:
   - An opportunity to discuss the problem(s)
   - Work toward a solution to the problem(s)
   - Reach a resolution that is agreeable to both of the disputants
   - The hearing will be confidential and all notes will be destroyed
4. Explain what a mediator is:
   - A neutral person who will not take sides
   - Mediator is there to help parties solve their problems
5. State the five rules again and ask both parties if they agree.
6. Ask both disputants to tell their side of the story and how they feel about what happened.
7. Paraphrase and listen actively to each disputant's side of the story and his or her feelings.
8. Ask each disputant to repeat back what the other said and how he or she felt.
9. Ask each disputant to tell what he or she could have done differently.
10. Paraphrase and listen actively to each disputant's response.
11. Ask each disputant what he or she could do right now to help solve the problem.
12. Paraphrase and listen actively to each disputant's response.
13. Help disputants find a solution they mutually feel good about.
14. Repeat the solution and all of its parts to each disputant and ask if each agrees.

Figure 8.2 An Outline for Peer Mediation

What is particularly noteworthy are the communication skills that define and permeate any good peer mediation program. For a peer mediator, listening accurately to the two disputants is critical to a successful resolution of a case.

After stating the problem and having each disputant express how he or she feels about it, the mediator can ask the parties active listening questions such as "So, _____ happened and then _____, and you're feeling _____, is that right?"

Often, having the peer mediator simply rephrase what each party has said and felt and ask each to repeat what the other has said and felt is an effective way of nudging one or both parties toward a resolution of the problem. The mediator can say things like "_____, tell us in your own words what you heard _____ say happened and how he or she is feeling" or "Even though you might not agree with _____, would you tell us what you heard him or her say?"

After each person is finished repeating what the other has said and felt, the mediator can ask each person, "_____, is that accurate? Do you want to add anything?"

In helping the disputants come up with solutions, the mediator can ask open-ended questions such as "What could you have done differently?" As each party responds, the mediator can again paraphrase and listen accurately.

Further questions that help the disputants come up with their own solution could include the following:

- "What do you want to do about this problem so it won't be a problem any more?"
- "What do you need to have happen so that this conflict will be resolved?"
- "Do you have any ideas about how to solve this problem?"
- "Is there any way we can reach an agreement?"
- "How would you like to see this settled?"
- "What do you want _____ to do or say so that this can be resolved?"
- "What would make you happy?"
- "What's important to you?"

Finally, in helping cement an agreement into place, the mediator will want to ask the following kinds of questions to make sure that both parties are happy about the suggested resolution:

- "Do you think this solution could work?"
- "Does this solve your problem?"
- "Will this solution work over time?"
- "Will this solution meet your needs?"
- "Is this a solution you can agree to?"

Developing a Successful Peer Mediation Program

Administrative Support

No program is successful without the active participation and involvement of the principal. Prior to embarking on the program, it is strongly recommended that the principal be oriented to the purpose of the program and involved, at some level, in all aspects of program implementation.

Selection of Students and Staff

There is an initial tendency to select the best and brightest students for an innovative program such as peer mediation. Unfortunately, conflicts are not limited to select students but occur at each grade level and within each academic and social group. Because students in conflict will be most comfortable relating to others they view as their peers, it is strongly recommended that students be selected from a cross-section of the school community. In general, three qualities appear to be associated with success as a peer mediator: a willingness to learn, good verbal skills, and having the respect of peers.

With respect to selecting staff, it is essential that at least one individual be assigned to coordinate and provide leadership for the program. This person should attend the training program with the students, work to develop procedures that make the program practical, and coordinate ongoing training for peer mediators.

Working in Pairs

Although some mediation programs require only one mediator to work with disputants, it is recommended that two mediators be assigned to each mediation. Particularly at the outset, this provides student mediators with a degree of confidence, knowing a fellow mediator is there for support.

Selling the Program

Even before training begins, it is helpful to provide inservice training for all staff members regarding the purposes of the program and how it can benefit the school community. This not only gives staff members an opportunity to have input into program training and procedures but also enables the administrator and trainer to identify staff members who may be interested in assisting with implementation.

Maintaining the Program

Once students, staff members, and parents have had training regarding the nature of the program and how it can benefit the school community, it is essential that an ongoing program of training, supervision, and evaluation be developed. Training might consist of periodic meetings in which peer mediators get together with the faculty supervisor to refresh skills and discuss problems that were encountered in mediation sessions. Supervision might consist of a faculty supervisor sitting in during mediation sessions to determine if additional training or supervision is needed.

It is essential that evaluation procedures be built into the program. Before leaving a mediation, each participant should be asked to evaluate the session in terms of whether an agreement was reached, whether the session was conducted fairly, and—even if an agreement was not reached—whether a better understanding of the issues was achieved. Data regarding the number of mediations held, the types of conflicts mediated, and the outcomes of mediation can be valuable tools in justifying continued resources from both within and outside the school community (Morse & Andrea, 1994).

Exercises in Conflict Resolution

1. Present to the faculty some basic alternatives-to-violence programs and see whether there is sufficient interest in pursuing further training sessions and start-up programs.

2. Ask a random selection of students how safe they feel at present in the school environment.

3. Contact other schools to see how they are handling violence and conflict in their schools.

4. Ask for teacher volunteers to begin some infusion into the classroom curriculum regarding conflict resolution programs and training in alternatives-to-violence programs.

5. Most important, during training role-play the steps of mediation in groups of three or four, depending upon whether you want to try it with comediators.

References

American Psychological Association. (1993). *Violence and youth.* Washington, DC: Public Interest Directorate.

Davis, A., & Porter, K. (1985). Tales of schoolyard mediation. *Update on Law Related Education,* Winter.

Johnson, C. (1995, March 27). 'Silent victims' who witness violence. *U.S. News & World Report,* pp. 29-30.

Johnson, D. W., Johnson, R.T., Dudley, B., & Burnett, R. (1992). Teaching students to be peer mediators. *Educational Leadership, 1,* 10-13.

Kort, C. (1990). Conflict resolution. *Boston Parents' Paper,* No. 7, 15, 26.

Levey, A. (1994, March 27). Voices of violence: Yearning for a safe world. *Cleveland Plain Dealer,* pp. C-4-C-5.

Morse, P. S., & Andrea, R. (1994). Peer mediation in the schools: teaching conflict resolution techniques to students. *NASSP Bulletin, 78*(560), 75-82.

Prothrow-Stith, D. (1991). *Deadly consequences.* New York: HarperCollins.

Sautter, R. C. (1995). Standing up to violence. *Phi Delta Kappan, 76*(5), K1-K12.

9

Integrating Communication Skills and Conflict Resolution Principles: A Model

Until this year, Elaine knew how to resolve conflict only by fighting back. She had been in two fights in the last 2 years. The most recent was with a classmate who kept calling her names and laughing at her worn-out shoes. Elaine talked to one of her friends, who suggested she should see a teacher-coordinator for the school's new peer mediation program. Elaine did. The teacher asked Elaine's tormentor if she would be willing to participate in a mediation session to help resolve the dispute, and 2 days later they met with two fellow students who comediated the session. The girls were able to come to a resolution and one more potential hot spot in the school was cleared away.

These are hopeful stirrings in the all-important context of how schools can foster caring and respect for their occupants; promote communication among teachers, students, administrators, and parents; and develop effective ways to solve problems and resolve conflicts.

There are those who suggest that schools should focus exclusively on the teaching of subject-matter basics and leave everything else to other institutions in society, but unless students, as well as teachers, feel safe, respected, and in contact with one another, the "holy curiosity of inquiry" becomes constricted, labored, and even strangled.

A Model Alternatives-to-Violence Program

Fortunately, there are an emerging number of efforts and programs that help promote such an environment. We would like to describe one model that incorporates many of the communication skills and conflict resolution principles we have discussed so far.

Alternatives to Violence in Schools (AViS) is a program presently being used in the Buffalo Public Schools in Buffalo, New York. Its structure revolves around a unique combination of caring and nurturing skills and exercises, the infusion of conflict-resolution principles and concepts into the curriculum, and the setting up of a peer mediation program in the participating school (Western New York Peace Center, 1996).

Behind the AViS program is the assumption, articulated and developed by John Dewey, that children become who they are through their social interactions. Dewey states,

> The only true education comes through the stimulation of the child's powers by the demands of the social situations in which he finds himself. Through these demands he is stimulated to act as a member of a unity, to emerge from his original narrowness of action and feeling, and to conceive of himself from the standpoint of the welfare of the group to which he belongs. Through the responses which others make to his own activities he comes to know what these mean in social terms. (Brown & Finn, 1988, p. 69)

Dewey's perspective on the relationship of the individual to the society has a counterpart in the relationship of the individual to the school. Schools are miniature societies, composed of groups of individuals who relate to the school through their social interactions. Developing a sense of belonging to a classroom group is a key factor in an individual's ability to do well in school. Conflict-resolution programs can promote that development of school community and membership of each individual in that community. Only when trust in the group is established, in fact, can peaceful relations really begin to be practiced (Stanford, 1977).

Too often, however, students do not experience the type of classroom community that can act as an alternative to the negative aspects of their larger social environment. Establishing school rules against fighting without establishing alternatives to a violent response to conflict will not suffice to change behaviors.

Students who participate in AViS become cognizant of alternative approaches to conflict in their lives. One stated, "I learned that instead of fighting I can talk about the problem and that there are a lot of alternatives to fighting." Another said, " I learned that a lot of us basically think alike. We all are antiviolent but because of the amount of violence around us, we are forced to react violently." AViS provides a positive social context within which students can learn what it means to interact with other individuals in a constructive, caring way, one that rejects violence as a way of dealing with conflicts in life.

Dealing With Attitudes: First Leg of the Program

One of the initial challenges in setting up an effective school conflict-resolution program is first to deal with and articulate one's attitudes toward violence and nonviolence and the program's immediate and visceral impact on the participants. Therefore, teachers, students, administrators, and sometimes parents who enroll in the AViS program initially go through a series of workshops based on the Alternatives to Violence Project (AVP). The latter began in 1975 in the New York State prison system and is still in place there. Its first workshop was held in Greenhaven Prison when an inmate group, the Think Tank, felt the need for nonviolence training in preparation for their upcoming roles as counselors in an experimental program in a Division for Youth institution for underage offenders. The Think Tank asked a local Religious Society of Friends (Quaker) group to provide such training. The result was the Alternatives to Violence Project. From Greenhaven, the program spread to other prisons, sometimes through prison Quaker meetings, more often by word of mouth. The effort has now spread to communities and prisons all across the country and is presently nonsectarian.

AVP has consistently tried to diminish the level of violence by reducing the need that people feel to resort to violence as a solution. The process uses the life experience of participants as a learning resource and draws on that experience to help participants deal constructively with the violence in themselves and in their lives.

Although the program originated in prisons, people soon discovered that the violence in prisons is merely a distilled version of the violence pervading the whole society, and that is why the program's message and practical content are universally applicable, not only to community groups and organizations but to schools as well (Alternatives to Violence Project, 1986, p. A-1).

In the AVP workshops, seven different areas are examined and reinforced through experiential, hands-on exercises; discussions; and small-group sharings. They are affirmation, community building, communication skills, consensus and decision making, cooperation, conflict resolution, and values and goals clarification.

A basic precept of AVP is the spirit of caring for all people. The workshops try to develop a sense of community in the group, based on respect for all the people in it. This is an important basis for developing means to finding nonviolent ways to deal with conflict.

Another fundamental assumption is that all people have some good points that can be built on and expanded as a way of transforming violent tendencies. As the workshops evolve from community building to conflict resolution, the focus moves toward the power everyone has to change a potentially violent situation into a peaceful settlement.

An important part of the workshops is to be open to looking at and talking about conflict and how the participants relate to and work through problems or disagreements. The workshops explore the benefits of working cooperatively together, rather than being in conflict or in competition with one another. Also, many activities focus on individual members examining their own and others' behavior to discover what increases and what decreases violence.

The workshops emphasize community and the development of trust and respect for one another in order to feel safe and secure together. In that spirit the participants are asked to observe the following ground rules:

1. Look for and affirm one another's good points.
2. Refrain from put-downs, both of yourself and of others.
3. Listen to what each person has to say; do not interrupt each other; do not speak too often or too long.
4. When volunteering, volunteer only yourself, not other people.
5. Observe confidentiality regarding the personal sharing of each participant. Nothing that is said is to be repeated outside the workshop.
6. Everyone has the right to pass at any time. (Alternatives to Violence Project, 1986, p. A-8)

Conflict-Resolution Curricula and Resources

The AVP workshops bring the members of the school closer together and help sensitize everyone to the basic human, personal, and attitudinal issues that confront all of us when we face conflict and violence. AVP fits nicely into the second leg of the AViS model, the infusion of conflict-resolution materials and resources into the curriculum. Fortunately, there is a wide array of options from which to choose. In fact, there has been a virtual explosion of resources available in the 10 years since the publication of one of the first "peace curricula" for classroom use (M. Finn & R. Murray, *Friendly Creature Features*, 1986, Western New York Peace Center, 2123 Bailey Ave., Buffalo, NY 14211, telephone 716-894-2013). Prior to and since then, many of the resource books have been in a "cookbook" style format, collections of activities and exercises for youth that cover many of the previously described themes of the AVP workshops.

The "grandmothers" of all such resource books are two Quaker-related publications by Priscilla Pritzman et al., *Friendly Classroom for a Small Planet*, produced by the Children's Creative Response to Conflict, 1988, and Stephanie Judson (Ed.), *A Manual on Nonviolence and Children*, Philadelphia, PA, 1984. Both these resources (first published in 1974 and 1977, respectively) can now be obtained from New Society Publishers, 4222 Baltimore Avenue, Philadelphia, PA 19143, telephone: 215-382-6543.

More recent and greatly expanded cookbook-type resources are Fran Schmidt and Alice Friedman, *Creative Conflict Solving for Kids (Grades 4-9),* better known as "Peaceworks," Grace Contrino Abrams Peace Education Foundation, Miami, FL, 1983, and William Kreidler, *Creative Conflict Resolution,* Scott Foresman Press, 1984. Recent publications by the Florida group include resource materials for both younger students and peer mediation programs. Write 2627 Biscayne Boulevard, Miami, FL 33137, or call 305-576-5075 for a catalog.

William Kreidler, who works for Educators for Social Responsibility (ESR) in Cambridge, MA has also prepared curricula for classroom use, published by ESR, including *Elementary Perspectives: Teaching Concepts of Peace and Conflict,* 1990. To obtain a listing of all ESR materials, write ESR, 23 Garden Street, Cambridge, MA 02138 or call 800-370-2515.

The New York City chapter of ESR, the Resolving Conflict Creatively Program (RCCP), working in conjunction with the Board of Education there, has developed the RCCP curricula for grades K-12. These resources are modeled on the AVP format and incorporate the AVP philosophy. The goals of the RCCP program are as stated: (a) to prepare educators across the country to provide high-quality instruction and effective school programs in conflict resolution and intergroup relations and (b) to transform the culture of participating schools so that they model values and principles of creative, nonviolent conflict resolution. The program's primary strategy is to reach young people by providing professional development for the adults in their lives—principals, teachers, and parents. Their materials, including their peer mediation resources, however, are available only along with their training. For information, write RCCP National Center, 163 Third Avenue, New York, NY 10003 or call 212-387-0225.

A West Coast organization that began with a peer mediation program and then expanded into classroom curricula is the Community Board Program in San Francisco. Their secondary school curriculum emphasizes communication skills and is an excellent companion to any mediation or conflict-resolution program. For a complete listing of all their resources, write The Community Board

Program, 1540 Market Street, Suite 490, San Francisco, CA 94102 or call 415-552-1250.

A product of the Committee for Children, Second Step is a violence-prevention program designed to reduce impulsive and aggressive behavior in children and increase their level of social competence. The program is composed of four curricula: preschool and kinder-garten, Grades 1-3, Grades 4-5, and Grades 6-8. Second Step teaches social and behavioral skills that tend to be lacking in high-risk children and in adult perpetrators of abuse. Among these skills are empathy, impulse control, and anger management. For further information or to view a 10-minute introductory video, contact Committee for Children, 2203 Airport Way South, Suite 500, Seattle, WA 98134-2027, or call 206-343-1223 or 800-634-4449.

More recently, the New Mexico Dispute Resolution Center has published a curriculum for teaching conflict resolution and peer mediation to adolescents. For information, write 620 Roma NW, Suite B, Albuquerque, NM 87102, or call 505-247-0571.

A medical doctor, Deborah Prothrow-Stith, has developed, with the assistance of William Kreidler, the *Violence Prevention Curriculum for Adolescents*, 1987. This resource and other materials are available from the Education Development Center, 55 Chapel Street, Newton, MA 02158, or call 617-969-7100, ext. 2215.

An Ohio group, PeaceGROWS, has a 20-session workshop for teachers and others who want to promote the concepts of conflict resolution and nonviolence in classrooms and other youth settings. An outline of the workshop sessions published by K. Bickmore et al., *Alternatives to Violence: A Manual for Teaching Peacemaking to Youth and Adults*, 1984, and other materials for classroom use are available from PeaceGROWS, 513 West Exchange Street, Akron, OH 44302, or call 216-864-5442.

As a final resource, the National Association for Mediation in Education (NAME) is a valuable resource for all who are involved in this work. They produce a newsletter, *The Fourth R*, and an extensive bibliography of materials that include most of the above as well as others. The address is 1726 M Street N.W., Suite 500, Washington, DC 20036-4502, and their telephone number is 202-466-4764, ext. 305.

A Peer Mediation Session

Finally, as a way of applying many of the skills of the first two parts of AViS and providing a structure in the school that actually ensures an effective alternative for dealing with conflicts, AViS works with the school in setting up an operational peer mediation program. Although we have already described some of the particulars of what goes into the training of peer mediators and the components of a program in chapter 8, we would like to provide a transcript of a peer mediation session as a way of showing the communication skills the mediators use and how a conflict is actually resolved.

The following involves a sixth-grade boy and girl who were involved in rumor spreading and "capping." The session involves two comediators and took place in the relative privacy of a "neutral" site on the school grounds. The microskills of the comediators are noted in parentheses. Also note that the five-stage interview model outlines the sessions:

Stage 1: Rapport and Structuring

Comediator 1: Hi. My name is Steve Stabler and I'm a peer mediator. (Self-disclosure)

Comediator 2: Hi. My name is Julie Brooks. (Self-disclosure)

Disputant 2: Hi. My name is Dori.

Disputant 1: My name is Jim. (All shake hands)

Comediator 1: These are the five rules that we ask you to agree to. The first rule is to be as honest as you can. Do you agree? (Information giving, concrete followed by check-out in form of a closed question)

Disputant 2: Yes. As long as he tells the truth.

Comediator 1: Do you agree not to interrupt? (Closed question)

Disputant 1: Yes. As long as she doesn't start capping on me.

Comediator 1: No name-calling or physical fighting. (Directive)

Disputant 1: Yes. I agree.

Disputant 2: I agree.

Comediator 1: Speak directly to us first? (Directive)

Disputants: Yes. (Note that the information given was very concrete and specific, the focus was on the problem, and a balance of information giving, directives, and closed questions was used to structure the session.)

Comediator 1: Do you agree to solve the problem?

Disputants: Yes.

Stage 2: Define the Problem

Comediator 1: Jim, why don't you tell your side of the story? (Open question, focus on Jim)

Disputant 1: Well, one of my friends told me that she spread a rumor about me that I wouldn't be able to get a girlfriend until I was 40. I didn't like that because it isn't true.

Comediator 1: O.K. You're saying that one of your friends told you that she spread a rumor that you wouldn't be able to find a girlfriend until you turned 40. How do you feel about that? (Paraphrase, open question oriented to feelings. We need emotions as well as facts for effective resolution of concerns.)

Disputant 1: I feel really angry because it's not true. My friends laugh at me because most of them have girlfriends and then she spreads a rumor that I don't, which I do.

Disputant 2: You shouldn't feel angry. I should feel angry because you keep insulting me.

Comediator 1: O.K. Let's not interrupt. (Directive)

Comediator 2: All right. What's your side of the story, Dori? (Open question, focus on Dori)

Disputant 2: I was walking in the hall and he had bumped into me and then he starts insulting me and then I say if you keep insulting me like this well then I'm going to tell the whole school the truth about you.

Comediator 2: Well, is it the truth? (Closed question)

Disputant 2: Well, it was a good way to get back at him.

Comediator 2: O.K. So you're saying that he bumped into you and he insulted you so you got mad and then you thought you should get back at him. How do you feel about it? (Paraphrase, open question oriented to feelings)

Disputant 2: I feel angry about this.

Comediator 2: Angry? (Minimal encourage)

Disputant 2: Because I was sick of him insulting me.

Comediator 2: O.K. (Minimal encourage)

Stages 3 and 4: Define Goals and Generate Solutions

Comediator 1: O.K. There are two problems here. There's one with the capping and this one with the rumors. Each of you feels angry and frustrated. We need two resolutions. Is there anything we can do? (Brief summary of the two points of view. In some cases, it would be wise to summarize each point of view in careful detail and make sure each disputant understands—or at least can repeat—the other person's point of view.)

Disputant 1: I can say excuse me next time.

Comediator 1: All right. (Minimal encourage)

Disputant 1: And apologize for my capping.

Comediator 1: Do you agree? (Closed question)

Disputant 2: Yes, I agree.

Comediator 2: What are you going to do about the rumors? (Open question)

Disputant 2: Well, I could tell everyone it wasn't true but first he has to say sorry to me.

Comediator 2: Is that O.K. with you? (Closed question)

Disputant 1: Yeah.

Stage 5: Commitment to Action

Comediator 1: All right. Do you think it's solved, this problem? (Closed question)

Disputant 1: No.

Comediator 1: What else? (Open question)

Disputant 1: I have to apologize.

Comediator 1: So apologize. (Directive)

Disputant 1: I apologize for my capping on you and being rude and next time I'll say excuse me.

Disputant 2: I accept your apology.

Comediator 1: Do you think your problem is over now? (Closed question)

Disputants: Yes.

Comediator 1: Good. Congratulations. Your problem is solved. (Minimal encourage, brief summary)

Disputants: O.K. (shake hands)

(Transcript from CNN Cable News Network.)

There are several things that are in evidence here. First, the disputants chose to sit down with the peer mediators rather than continuing the dispute among themselves. The mediators reviewed the rules and also reminded the disputants when they were breaking them. For example, when Dori interrupted Jim at one point, one of the comediators reminded her not to interrupt.

Both mediators used paraphrasing, and Steve summarized what the dispute was about when both disputants had finished explaining their side of the conflict. Both mediators also engaged in open-ended questions and also asked the disputants to reflect their feelings after telling their respective stories. Also, the mediators affirmed the disputants by congratulating them on solving the problem.

The five-stage interview model illustrates that mediation is a problem-solving structure. Often, disputes can escalate if each stage is not honored fully. Needless to say, more complex issues require considerably more attention to defining clear goals and to generating alternative resolutions.

The presence of a peer mediation program also offers a more subtle but equally powerful element to the school. In the students' social circles word soon gets around of the presence of this new "approach" to discipline. And if taken seriously by the school community, some important modeling soon begins to take hold: the mediators themselves now possess new skills and status and can begin using them not only during actual campus disputes, but also among their friends and family. And the disputants themselves will experience a new way to resolve a conflict that certainly feels better than engaging in a fight, with its attendant anxieties and simmering and unresolved emotions that both the victor and the vanquished continue to carry around.

A successful peer mediation program is a way of translating efforts like AVP and sound conflict-resolution curricula into a rational, alternative approach to discipline. The former completes the loop in providing the necessary concepts, attitudes, and skills for an effective conflict-management program in the schools.

You also may have noted that the brief example here would serve as a useful framework for adult disputes—those involving parents, teachers, or administrative conflict. The same skills and mediation structures apply.

Final Thoughts

As we look at the uncertain and sometimes perilous environment of the schools, we must continue to believe that we have the power to change this environment. The single statement of a student continues to haunt us. In reviewing with us her daily struggles, she said, "I try so hard but there seems so much out there that you just have to put up with."

Structural causes of violence are largely out of our control. However, a clearer understanding of the sources of violence over which we do have some control and the assumption of responsibility for these things help to give us some working space. Although lack of employment, commercialism, and media exploitation are institutional, nonindividual sources of violence, events like unplanned pregnancies, drug use, and violent reactions to anger are conscious choices that can be controlled with proper support, guidance, and encouragement (Brady, 1995).

Bronfenbrenner (*Investing in Our Children*, 1980) states that what is needed for a child to develop emotionally, socially, and morally is participation in progressively more complex joint activities on a regular basis and over an extended period of time with one or more persons with whom the child develops a strong, mutual, irrational emotional attachment. Brendtro and Long (1995) also affirm that the most powerful restraints on violent behavior—because they meet children's most basic need—are healthy human attachments in a consistent, safe, loving environment. Although we would hope that children have that first and foremost with their families, it can also be with a teacher or other adult with whom a child comes in contact.

Again, we cannot expect children to learn nonviolent conflict resolution unless we model it ourselves. As parents, teachers, and administrators we need to apply these communicative concepts to our own lives. Until we apply these ideas to ourselves, our family and our work and play lives, we cannot expect more from children.

Although not all of us as teachers and administrators can fully provide that irrational tie that children need, we can help create a more caring, humane, safe, and inviting environment for our students. The application of communication skills and the use of conflict-resolution principles can go a long way toward producing schools that do provide the joyful, emotional, and intellectually stimulating places that all of us want for our students. How to get there and by what means remains the challenge for all of us.

References

Alternatives to Violence Project, Inc. (1986). *Manual: Basic course.* New York: Alternatives to Violence Project.

Brady, E. M. (1995). How to survive urban violence with hope. *English Journal, 84*(5), 43-50.

Brendtro, L., & Long, N. (1995). Breaking the cycle of violence. *Educational Leadership, 52*(5), 52-56.

Brown, S. I., & Finn, M. E. (Eds.). (1988). *Readings from progressive education.* Lanham, MD: University Press of America.

CNN Cable News Network. *Conflict managers in action.* The Community Board Program, Inc. (Conflict resolution resources for schools and youth.)

Investing in our children. (1980). Washington, DC: Hearing before the Subcommittee on Education and Health of the Joint Economic Committee of the House and Senate (testimony of U. Bronfenbrenner).

Stanford, G. (1977). *Developing effective classroom groups.* New York: Hart.

Western New York Peace Center. (1996). *Alternatives to violence in schools.* Buffalo, NY: Author.